MARLBOROUGH AND HIS CAMPAIGNS

1702-1709.

With the Battles described in conjunction with Field Service Regulations, Vol. II., by the kind permission of the Controller of H.M. Stationery Office.

BY

A. KEARSEY, D.S.O., O.B.E., p.s.c.

LATE LIEUTENANT-COLONEL, GENERAL STAFF

The Naval & Military Press Ltd

Published by

The Naval & Military Press Ltd
Unit 5 Riverside, Brambleside
Bellbrook Industrial Estate
Uckfield, East Sussex
TN22 1QQ England

Tel: +44 (0)1825 749494

www.naval-military-press.com
www.nmarchive.com

CONTENTS

INTRODUCTION.

THE author has endeavoured, after a study of some of the leading authorities, to write down, with judgment and impartiality, his deductions and comments on the four principal battles in Marlborough's Campaigns, 1702-1709.

The author hopes that these comments may prove helpful to those who have not had the time for extensive research and who wish to have the main points presented to them in a complete and concise form. The works which have been consulted on Marlborough and his campaigns are by Coxe, Taylor, Lediard, and Wolseley. The wars of Marlborough are of great interest, on account of the military science displayed by this skilful and bold commander. He was a successful commander, and the study of the psychology of success is important for all soldiers.

Marlborough's successes were attained by making his plan on the best information obtainable after close personal reconnaissances of the enemy's positions. Then, by always being in a forward position throughout his battles, where he could see for himself the situations and developments, he detected any weak points in the enemy's dispositions or operations, and he directed there a decisive attack, and maintained the impetus and offensive power of his troops until he had gained a victory. Thus at Malplaquet on September 11th, 1709, directly the French commander had weakened his centre in the Trouée d'Aulnois, he sent Orkney to attack the French lines there with all available men. Once their centre was broken, Boufflers was unable to retrieve the disaster, and the whole French Army was forced to retreat. At Oudenarde, on July 11th, 1708, directly Marlborough saw that Vendôme had not occupied the dominating height, Boser Couter, on his right flank, he sent Overkirk with all the troops that could be spared from his left flank and centre to occupy it.

Once on this hill, the line of retreat of the French right flank was threatened, and their position became untenable. Darkness only saved the French Army from annihilation or capture.

At Ramillies, on May 23rd, 1706, Marlborough saw that the concave position occupied by the French between Autréglise and Taviers would enable him to bring troops more quickly to the centre than his enemy could. He realized that, by piercing the French centre and by occupying the Tomb of Ottomond, he would make the French position untenable, and he would gain a decisive victory.

Accordingly, he made a feint against Autréglise while he attacked Taviers and Ramillies. The feint was successful, as the French commander weakened his right and centre to meet it.

Marlborough then pressed through after heavy fighting at Ramillies and south of it with all available strength to the Tomb of Ottomond, which commanded the whole plain north of the River Mehaigne.

The French commander then saw that the result of the battle was decided, and gave orders for retreat. At Blenheim, on August 13th, 1704, as soon as Marlborough noted that the French position was weakly held by cavalry between Blenheim and Oberglauheim, he stopped his frontal attack against these villages, and sent his cavalry, guns, and infantry across the River Nebel against the French centre. They were able to break through the thinly held lines in their front, and then to advance in a south-westerly direction, driving all the troops in front of them and the River Danube back upon that river. This operation gave Marlborough a complete and decisive victory.

Marlborough, too, had a strong and arresting personality. In his private life—which is more important than any public reputation—there were the same patience and self-control that enabled him to deal successfully with jealous and suspicious allies, and to command their armies.

At a time when his contemporaries were for the most part coarse and profligate, he was a devoted and faithful husband, and not even his greatest enemies—Thackeray and Swift—have been able truly to dispute this fact. There is never any complaint in his writings as to his wife's somewhat boisterous temper, which at times must have been trying to a man who was naturally fastidious and dignified. His affection for his daughters was amply repaid.

Immorality and indelicate boasting in speech and writings were fashionable in his day, but he was invariably courteous to women, and his speech and writings were simple and restrained. His fear of poverty, and his personal ambition, led him into errors that were later redeemed by giving all his time and energy to the service of his country.

His early frailties were, to some extent, counter-balanced by his whole-hearted, steadfast devotion to his family, and by his chivalry to his Queen. Throughout his life his letters show that he was deeply religious.

During his life he had the satisfaction of obtaining fame, riches and an autocratic power over others. But, in addition, he gained the great conquest and the enduring form of power, which were won by his knowledge and mastery of self.

He records that, before his battles, there were prayers for the troops, and he himself received the Sacrament, however early he had to start. After his victories, again on his knees, we read, that he gave the praise and acknowledgment where they were due. His letters show that he realized that all his achievements were the result of divine gifts, and that he was a humble instrument in an Almighty purpose, which enabled him to develop all that was best in himself; and, by his sincere faith and constant prayer, he was able to meet flattery and abuse, fame and temporary loss of royal favour with equal composure and serenity.

At moments of the greatest difficulty he never lost his self-control. He was constantly thwarted and hampered in his campaigns by the Dutch Deputies.

In 1703, he could have captured Antwerp and Ostend. On August 16th, 1705, he threatened Brussels from the south, and was prevented from winning a great victory at Waterloo.

In 1707, near Nivelles, he was prevented from bringing the French to an engagement. On August 30th, 1708, when the French Army, under Berwick and Vendôme, retired in the direction of Oudenarde from their positions between Lessines and Grammont, Marlborough would have followed them up and defeated them, but the Dutch Deputies refused to allow this movement to take place.

He bore these interferences with the greatest possible patience. He was constantly faced by the dubious alternatives which abound in all wars and battles, but his strong and resolute will and clear judgment enabled him to make decisions and to carry them through.

In turn, Tallard at Blenheim, Villeroy and the Elector of Bavaria at Ramillies, Vendôme and Burgundy at Oudenarde, Villars and Boufflers at Malplaquet were dominated and defeated by his great resolution. Our Regulations tell us that " Leadership requires personal courage, high intelligence, sound judgment, an intuitive faculty and great resolution." These qualities Marlborough abundantly possessed.

At Oberglauheim, on August 13th, 1704, he restored the battle; at Ramillies he rode in front of and rallied the Dutch, and then led the final charge which carried the village of Ramillies, and decided the day in favour of the Allies.

It was Marlborough at Oudenarde who led the left wing of his army, and, when he had driven the French back from

Browaan, was able to give the orders for the defeat of the French Army. At Malplaquet, when the impatience and disobedience of the Prince of Orange on his left flank had endangered his plan of operations, he intervened personally to restore the battle at the head of some Prussian and Hanoverian battalions, which he had been able to collect.

We find in Marlborough a combination of determination and piety, of courage and devotion to his family, as well as a deep and abiding faith, which enabled him to develop his aptitude for patience, his consummate sense of proportion, and his transcendent capacity for taking trouble; and thus to achieve, by his sound judgment and resolution, victory over France and Louis XIV.

He became one of England's greatest servants, and one who has an undying claim on our gratitude.

MARLBOROUGH AND HIS CAMPAIGNS
1702-1709.

CHAPTER I.

DIARY OF EVENTS—1650-1701.

JOHN CHURCHILL, afterwards Duke of Marlborough, was born on June 5th, 1650. In September, 1667, he was gazetted as an Ensign in the Grenadier Guards. He first saw service in Tangier from 1668 to 1670, attached to the Queen's Regiment in the operations against the Moors. He then returned to the household of the Duke of York, where, as Macaulay says, " he was early distinguished as a man of fashion and of pleasure. His stature was commanding, his face handsome, his address singularly winning, his temper, even under the most vexatious and irritating circumstances, always under perfect command."

However, in justice to Churchill it must be noted that he abandoned his life of fashion and pleasure whenever he had an opportunity of being on active service. The next opportunity he had was in the naval action, in June, 1672, at the Battle of Southwold Bay. Here he was on board the Duke of York's flagship with his company of Grenadiers.

He gained experience of the difficulties and peculiarities of naval warfare in this tactically indecisive action. For his good services in this action—in which he remained on the crippled battleship from which the Duke of York had to transfer his flag—he was promoted to the rank of Captain.

Shortly afterwards, his company was again under orders for active service. He was sent over to France in December, 1672, in a contingent commanded by the Duke of Monmouth, for the service of Louis XIV against the Dutch, in accordance with the secret Treaty of Dover.

The main terms of this treaty must be considered, as otherwise it is difficult to understand how England became involved in this Continental war. Charles II agreed to help the French against the Dutch, in return for £300,000 and the possibility of receiving the province of Zealand and adjacent islands if the war was successful. He was to have £200,000 a year if he became a Catholic. In addition, he was to have at his disposal thirty French ships for naval operations against de Ruyter's fleet.

B

Churchill distinguished himself at Maestricht, in June, 1674, by his personal gallantry and initiative in helping to capture and hold one of the outworks of this besieged town.   He saved the life of the Duke of Monmouth at the siege of Maestricht.   Louis XIV complimented him on his valour.

He then served with Turenne in Germany, and learned the methods which made this famous soldier so successful. Turenne put into practice the principle of manœuvring while on the march and before gaining contact with an enemy, in order to combine frontal and flank attacks.   Turenne also realized the necessity of having a large proportion of infantry in an army.   From this time, infantry became the predominant arm in battle.   The triangular, locking-ring bayonet was a cause for this.   Its introduction enabled the musketeer to do without the pikemen to defend himself and then to take the offensive after the fire fight.   Infantry now combined protection with mobility and offensive action.

Shortly after Turenne's death, three-quarters of the French Army were composed of infantry.   Armies began to occupy a more extended frontage in proportion to their numbers. Infantry were armed with musket and bayonet, and the pike was abolished.

The front of a battalion, when deployed for action in three ranks, was increased owing to the abolition of the phalanx formation for pikemen.   Owing to the increased frontages and additional power of manœuvre, and owing to the nature of the country, reconnaissance and entrenchments became increasingly important factors in operations.   At both Blenheim and Ramillies, Marlborough demonstrated this evolution in tactical principles by manœuvring after gaining information as to the ground in his front, the obstacles to his advance, and the vulnerable point against which he could concentrate superior numbers.

At Blenheim, he was able to restore the cause of the Emperor in Germany after a well-planned march into Bavaria, and at Ramillies he regained Flanders for the Archduke, in spite of treachery and the surrender of Ghent and Bruges on his communications.   At Blenheim, the French held the villages strongly, but the intervals were weakly defended.

Marlborough made full use of this knowledge to cross the River Nebel at unguarded points with a force of all arms, and pushed on to the River Danube,   At Ramillies, as one wing was behind a marsh which was impassable, Marlborough concentrated against the other wing and defeated it.

By the end of 1673, he had been promoted to the rank of Lieutenant-Colonel.   In February, 1674, peace with Holland was concluded.   Churchill was appointed to command a regiment of a British contingent in the French service for a campaign under Turenne in this year (1674).

The British infantry took a creditable part, on June 16th, 1674, in the brilliant victory at Sinsheim, which Turenne gained over Bournonville, and by which he regained Alsace for Louis XIV.

Later, on October 4th in this year, Churchill again distinguished himself in the fight for Little Woods at the Battle of Entzheim.

Also at Turckheim, in January, 1675, the British infantry, in which Churchill was still commanding a regiment, was prominent.   This victory led to the evacuation of Lorraine by the Elector of Brandenburg, and the British contingent was able to go into winter quarters at Metz.

Throughout these months of fighting under Turenne, Churchill gained valuable experience.   Turenne's strategy was as daring as his tactics were bold and skilful.   He had, by means of determined leading, illustrated how offensive action and mobility and surprise can compensate for numerical inferiority.   One of Turenne's great merits was to show how positions could be passed by manœuvring.

Churchill remained in the service of the French till 1677, when he was promoted to the rank of Colonel of a regiment of foot.   In the winter of this year, he married Sarah Jennings, one of the Maids of Honour to the Duchess of York.   Macaulay makes the following interesting statement about Sarah Jennings:

" Among the gallants who sued for her favour, Colonel Churchill, young, handsome, graceful, insinuating, eloquent, and brave, obtained the preference.   He must have been enamoured indeed.   For he had little property except the annuity which he had bought with the infamous wages bestowed on him by the Duchess of Cleveland; he was insatiable of riches: Sarah was poor.   His love after a struggle prevailed over his avarice; marriage only strengthened his passion; and to the last hour of his life Sarah enjoyed the pleasure and distinction of being the one human being who was able to mislead that far-sighted and sure-footed judgment, who was fervently loved by that cold heart, and who was servilely feared by that intrepid spirit.   In a worldly sense the fidelity of Churchill was amply rewarded.   His bride, though slenderly portioned, brought with her a dowry which, judiciously employed, made him at length a Duke of England, a

Prince of the Empire, the captain-general of a great coalition, the arbiter between mighty princes, and, what he valued more, the wealthiest subject in Europe."

This last sentence may be a little exaggerated.   Churchill had great gifts.   He had sound judgment, patience, determination, and considerable diplomatic and military ability, which must have brought him advancement among contemporaries who, for the most part, were vicious and idle.

In addition, his pleasant manners, his tact, and his unfailing good temper made him popular.   To the list of his good qualities must be added physical courage, and it is then possible to realize that military success and fame were within his grasp.

Another historian has told us of other qualities, that

" He was a skilful negotiator, he had a most insinuating and persuasive eloquence, which prevailed over the most prejudiced judgments; for a time it enabled him to hold almost absolute sway over the States-General, the Parliament and the Queen.   Even Eugène yielded to the Duke on several important occasions when their opinions differed.   As a soldier, he combined the greatest activity with a bravery which Turenne and Louis XIV admired on more than one occasion.   Endowed with a certain *coup d'œil*, he perceived the least faults of his enemies, and knew always how to take advantage of them.   Few generals have been so fortunate; he was always victorious and never suffered any serious check.   He was beloved by his soldiers because he took excellent care of them, although he did not spare their blood when occasion required, and he maintained in his camp the strictest discipline; for him they would gladly run into the greatest dangers."

In January, 1678, Charles announced that he had made an alliance with the Dutch to protect Flanders against the French. Churchill now became occupied with work which had a most important bearing on his future.   He was employed on negotiations with William of Orange as to the employment of the British contingent in Holland.

In September, 1678, he was given a brigade in Monmouth's contingent for service with the Army in Flanders.   The Peace of Nimuegen, however, put an end to hostilities, and Churchill returned to England early in 1679.

During the next three years, he was engaged in many secret missions for the Duke of York with Charles II and with Louis XIV.   For these services he was created Baron

Churchill on December 31st, 1682.   In November, 1683, he was given the command of the Royal Dragoons.

The next active service for Churchill was the suppression of the Monmouth Rebellion in 1685.   He was made a Brigadier and given command of eight troops of cavalry and five companies of infantry.

By June 27th, Churchill had collected his main body at Bath, and he had followed up and harassed Monmouth's troops, who were driven back to Philip's Norton.   Feversham, however, had superseded him in his command, and operations were now not so vigorously continued as they had been by Churchill. On July 15th, owing to Churchill's energetic handling of his troops at Sedgmoor, Monmouth's force was defeated; and the rebellion shortly afterwards came to an end.   Marlborough was promoted to the rank of Major-General.   James's position on the throne was now secure.

The general feeling throughout the country soon became so hostile to James's Roman Catholic views that, on June 30th, 1688, a letter was sent to William of Orange, asking him to bring an army to England and secure the liberties of the people.   This letter was signed, among others, by the Bishop of London, Devonshire, Shrewsbury, Danby, Lumley, and Compton.

Accordingly, William decided that he would bring an army to secure a free and legal Parliament, by whose decision he would abide.   On November 5th, 1688, William landed at Torbay and marched to Exeter.   Danby and Devonshire raised an insurrection in the North.   Churchill and many officers deserted James, and brought over to William's cause some of their troops.   Churchill clearly saw that, if James remained on the throne, all who did not become Roman Catholics must be ruined.

In this connection, it is interesting to quote Macaulay's views of Churchill's conduct.   He brings out clearly the motive which inspired Churchill throughout his life.   It is only fair to state that, though self-interest and self-advancement seem to have been his aims, yet the standard of morality in those days in the courts of the Stuarts was terribly low :

" He had been raised to eminence and from poverty to wealth.   Having started in life a needy ensign, he was now, in his 37th year, a Major-General, a peer of Scotland, a peer of England; he commanded a troop of Life Guards; he had been appointed to several honourable and lucrative offices; and as yet there was no sign that he had lost any part of the favour to which he owed so much.   He was bound to James, not only by the common obligations of allegiance, but by military honour, by personal gratitude, and, as appeared to superficial observers, by the strongest ties of interest.

" But Churchill was no superficial observer.   He knew exactly what his interest really was.   If his master were only at full liberty to employ Papists not a single Protestant would be employed.   Churchill might indeed secure himself from this danger and might raise himself still higher in the royal favour, by conforming to the Church of Rome.   A terrible alternative was before him.   The earthly evil which he most dreaded was poverty.   The one crime from which his heart recoiled was apostasy.   And if the designs of the Court succeeded, he could not doubt that between poverty and apostasy he must soon make his choice.

" And thus this man, who had owed his rise to his sister's dishonour, who had been kept by the most profuse, imperious, and shameless of harlots, and whose public life, to those who can look steadily through the dazzling blaze of genius and glory will appear a prodigy of turpitude, believed implicitly in the religion which he had learned as a boy, and shuddered at the thought of formally abjuring it."

James left the kingdom on December 23rd, 1688.   William and Mary, having accepted the Declaration of Right, were declared King and Queen on February 13th, 1689.   Churchill was now employed in reorganizing the Army.   In this capacity it is reported that he added to his income by receiving bribes for commissions and for contracts.   But the inefficient state of the Army in Ireland for the next two years cannot be laid to Churchill's account entirely.   The Army had to be enlarged rapidly, and consequently there was not time for complete supervision of all details in interior economy and in the selection of officers.

In this year, war was declared against France on May 15th.   Churchill had now been created the Earl of Marlborough, and in June was given the command of the British forces in the Netherlands, consisting of about 8,000 men, under the command of the Prince of Waldeck.   On August 27th, at the Battle of Walcourt, twelve miles south of Charleroi, Marlborough greatly distinguished himself by his gallantry and skill in leading his cavalry against the flank of the attacking French troops when they had succeeded in driving back our Allies holding one side of the village.

Marlborough was appointed to command the troops in Ireland after the Battle of the Boyne.

On October 1st, 1690, he reached Cork Harbour in command of 10,000 men.   By October 26th, he had compelled the garrisons of Cork and Kinsale to capitulate.

Marlborough then organized further plans of campaign in Ireland until, in the following year, he was sent to the Netherlands to assemble the forces for a campaign against Louis XIV.

However, on January 20th, 1692, he was suspected of treason and dismissed from all his offices.   It was not until May 15th that he was arrested and sent to the Tower.   On his release, he lived for nearly four years in retirement.   During this time, he corresponded with King James, with a view to service with him.

The war under King William was not successfully carried out.   He was defeated at Steinkirk in 1692, and at Landen in July, 1693.   After our defeat at Brest in 1694, Marlborough offered his services to King William.

He received no further employment, however, until 1698, when he was appointed to be the Governor of the Household to the nineteen-year-old son of Anne.   He now became more intimate with King William.

1700.—Charles II of Spain died.   Then Louis XIV placed his son's second son on the Spanish throne and took possession of Belgium in violation of the Partition Treaty, by which the Spanish Dominions were to be divided between France and Austria.

1701.—In June, the Commons, at William's request, agreed to assist him and his Allies in maintaining the liberty of Europe.   Twelve battalions were ordered to embark for Holland from Ireland; Marlborough was appointed to command them, and also he was to act as Ambassador Extraordinary and Plenipotentiary to the United Provinces.

At this point, when Marlborough was in command of a force, it may be well to note the organization of European armies during his wars.   The artillery was not considered as a tactical unit of organization.   Owing to the predominant part played by siege warfare, heavy artillery was improved, but there was little progress in the use of field artillery.   At Oudenarde, the artillery on either side was freely used.   The main arms were infantry and cavalry.   During a battle, the guns were, as a rule, arranged among the troops, and then, after the action was over, they were taken back to their own areas, or parks as they were called.

Infantry was in battalions of thirteen companies, each fifty strong, armed with muskets and socket bayonets. They were formed up in four ranks. The cavalry was organized on a basis of one horse-soldier to three foot-soldiers.

A squadron consisted of four companies, each of thirty-five men. In forming up for battle, the centre was normally composed of infantry, with cavalry on both wings. Behind this formation was a reserve of a few battalions and squadrons.

In those days, there was very little manœuvre or change of formation to meet contingencies and changing conditions during a battle. Opposing armies deliberately formed up facing each other in parallel bodies, and then they entrenched. Marlborough introduced manœuvre, and transferred troops to a spot in the enemy's lines where success might lead to decisive results.

Cavalry tactics in this period did not advance. Speed of action was not fully used. At Blenheim, 8,000 sabres charged through the centre of the French line, but their pace was at a trot. The charge was successful, because the French did not think that the marshy ground they crossed was passable for cavalry.

An offensive treaty against France was signed between England and Holland in September, 1701. King James II died on the day on which it was made. Louis XIV acknowledged James's son as heir to the throne. The reply to this by the Houses of Parliament was to arrange a Bill of Attainder against the Pretender, and to make preparations for war.

William III, the Dutch, and Germans began to consider the necessity of taking up arms against France.

CHAPTER II.

King William died on March 19th. Shortly before his death, he recommended to Queen Anne that Marlborough should command the Army in the Netherlands in the war against France. England, Holland, the German Empire, Hanover, and Prussia took up arms against France, whose allies were Spain, Bavaria, Portugal, and Savoy. This war of the Spanish Succession was fought on the north of France in Flanders, on her eastern frontier on the Rhine and in Germany, on the south-east in the Valley of the River Po, and on the south in Spain.

Anne, shortly after her accession, invested Marlborough with the Order of the Garter, and made him Captain-General of H.M. Forces. He was sent over to Holland as an Ambassador, and appointed Commander-in-Chief there for the Armies of the Alliance.

His difficulties were as much diplomatic as military. He had to deal with a coalition whose conflicting interests made them difficult and jealous. He found that the Dutch were selfish and that the Germans were formal and disinclined to carry out any original ideas. He displayed in a quite remarkable degree a knowledge of human nature, good temper, and tact. For instance, in spite of Dutch stubbornness and protests, in 1702 he crossed the River Meuse and operated in the Spanish Netherlands.

He captured Venloo, Ruremonde, and Liège. He cut off the French from the Lower Rhine. He overran the Electorate of Cologne, the Bishopric of Liège, and the Duchy of Limburg.

Particular Dates—1702.

May 5th.—War was declared against France. At this time, the French had the advantage in position and numbers. They had 90,000 men available for operations, and, except for the town of Maestricht, where the Dutch had 10,000 men, they were in occupation of the River Meuse between Namur and Venloo, and also of the Electorate of Cologne, and also of Spanish Flanders.

For operations on the Meuse, the French Army of 60,000 was commanded by Marshal Boufflers. The Allies had 25,000 men under Lord Athlone in the vicinity of Cleves, thirty miles north of Venloo.

June 10th was the date of the first operation in Dutch Brabant. Boufflers made a raid on Nimuegen, the base of the Allies' Army. Athlone moved his troops back by a night march, and reached his base just ahead of Boufflers. His rearguard, formed by British battalions, effectively kept off the French, who, when they were met on arrival in the vicinity of Nimuegen with fire from the guns manned by the burghers of this town, withdrew back to the River Rhine, some ten miles in a southerly direction. Athlone then retired with his force north of the River Waal.

July 2nd.—Marlborough left the Hague to take command of the Allied Forces, now up to a strength of 60,000, of which 12,000 were British, divided into three brigades; also he had 104 guns. He was accompanied by two Dutch Deputies.

July 26th.—Marlborough crossed the Meuse below Grave to the south bank preparatory to forcing the French from the country north-west of Cleves.

July 30th.—Marlborough's army reached the vicinity of Halmont, twenty miles south of Grave.

July 31st.—Marlborough's army reached the vicinity of St. Hubert's Lille. Boufflers now became alarmed, and began to conform to the Allies' offensive operations. He called in his forces under Tallard from the Rhine, and pushed on towards Venloo.

August 2nd.—Boufflers' army reached a position between the towns of Peer and Bray (seven miles south of St. Hubert's Lille). The Dutch Deputies would not allow Marlborough to make an attack on the French.

August 5th.—Boufflers, after a night march, crossed the River Demer at Diest. Here he was joined by Tallard. The Spanish Netherlands were now freed of the French. Marlborough brought the garrison of Maestricht to his field army.

August 9th.—Boufflers marched north to try to cut off a convoy marching from Grave to join Marlborough.

August 12th.—Marlborough marched back towards Hamont to meet his convoy.

August 22nd.—Marlborough reached the vicinity of Helchteren and was thus astride Boufflers' line of retreat to the River Demer. Boufflers formed up for battle. In spite of the fact that the French were tired and disorganized, and their power of manœuvre was restricted by the marshes on their left flank, the Dutch Deputies would not allow Marlborough to attack, as they considered it was too late in the day, although his orders for it had been issued.

August 23rd.—Boufflers' main body retreated to a position on the River Demer.   Our 3rd Dragoon Guards charged and dispersed the French rearguards, but the Allies were unable to get into touch with their main body.

August 28th.—The French were at Moll and Baelen.

August 29th.—The French had now withdrawn from the River Meuse.   Marlborough began the investment of Venloo. This siege lasted for eighteen days.

September 17th.—Venloo fell after the British troops had captured the outlying forts.

October 5th.—Stevenswaert capitulated to the Allies.

October 7th.—Ruremonde, at the junction of the Roer and Meuse, surrendered to the Allies after an eight days' siege. Marshal Tallard, with a large force, was sent back to guard Cologne and Bonn.

October 12th.—Boufflers marched his force, weakened by the loss of Tallard's detachment, to Liège.   Here Marlborough was waiting for him.   The Dutch Deputies would not allow Marlborough to attack the French, who were able to escape by a night march to Landen, twenty-four miles north-west of Liège.

October 23rd.—Liège surrendered to Marlborough, who had now gained possession of the whole line of the River Meuse from Liège to the sea.

December 9th.—Marlborough returned to London.   His operations, in spite of Dutch interference, had been most successful and encouraging.

December 25th.—For his services, Marlborough was made a Duke, and was awarded a pension of £5,000 a year.

CHAPTER III.

1703—General Summary of Events.

During this year, the Dutch considerably hampered Marlborough's plans, otherwise he would have taken Antwerp and Ostend. Marlborough wished to take advantage of his superiority of numbers in the Netherlands, by attacking the French lines between the Mehaigne and the Leuwe. The Dutch Deputies would not consent to this, as they could not realize that the French armies were their main objectives. The French, on the other hand, made a better use of their superiority of numbers in Bavaria, as Villars defeated the Allies' field army there. However, Marlborough was able to secure Holland from invasion by capturing Bonn on the Rhine, and Huy and Limburg on the Meuse.

Particular Dates—1703.

March 17th.—Marlborough returned to the Hague. His plan was to take the offensive in French Flanders and Brabant. The Dutch, however, overruled this, and he had to start his campaign with the siege of Bonn.

His immediate enemy in the Netherlands was a force of approximately 60,000 men under Marshal Villeroy, in the vicinity of Antwerp and Bruges. The French had, during the previous autumn, been successful in their operations on the Upper Rhine.

April 13th.—Marlborough arrived at Maestricht. His force was now forty battalions and sixty squadrons.

April 27th.—Marlborough's force, consisting of forty battalions and sixty squadrons, marched to Bonn to besiege it. He left a small covering force between Liège and Maestricht.

April 28th.—The French under Villeroy marched against the Allies' covering force, and were checked at Tongres by a Dutch and a British battalion, who held this place.

April 29th.—The garrison of Tongres capitulated to the French.

May 4th.—Villeroy advanced towards the Allies' covering force, now close to Maestricht.

May 15th.—Villeroy withdrew.

May 17th.—Bonn fell.

May 18th.—Marlborough returned to his covering force at Maestricht. His plan now was to make simultaneous advances both into Brabant and into West Flanders. He meant to capture Antwerp and Ostend. The English fleet was to co-operate and to distract the enemy's attention by threatening to land troops at Dieppe.

May 25th.—Marlborough, with sixty battalions and 120 squadrons, crossed the River Jaar. The French retired on Huy. Marlborough now decided to operate near Antwerp.

June 9th.—Marlborough's plan failed owing to Cohorn, the Dutch commander, taking his force into West Flanders to raid the country for contributions instead of attacking Ostend.

June 20th.—Marlborough decided to march to the vicinity of Lierre, ten miles south-east of Antwerp.

June 26th.—Opdam, one of the Dutch commanders, who was to co-operate with other Dutch forces under Spaar and Cohorn, marched to Eckeren, just north of Antwerp, where he was out of touch with the other columns.

June 30th.—Opdam was defeated by the French at Eckeren. He withdrew to Breda, leaving his second-in-command to endeavour to extricate his force. Half of his force, however, was compelled to surrender.

July 5th.—Marlborough went to Breda to see the Dutch Deputies and to arrange for the attack on Villeroy's position between Lierre and Antwerp.

July 12th.—Villeroy left his position. Marlborough was ready to attack, but the Dutch, who were to co-operate, were late in coming up to the scene of action. Before a concerted attack by the Allies could be arranged, Villeroy withdrew behind his lines again. The Dutch then refused to attack.

July 24th.—Marlborough had to change his plans owing to the refusal by the Dutch to attack Villeroy's army. He decided to return to the River Meuse and attack Huy, in order to force the French to detach troops to cover Namur.

August 3rd.—Marlborough started his return journey.

August 5th.—Marlborough's army crossed the River Demer at Hasselt.

August 16th.—Huy was invested.

August 25th.—Huy was captured.   The two battalions which had capitulated on April 29th at Tongres were released by the French, in accordance with the terms of surrender of Huy.   Marlborough now decided to invest Limburg (seventeen miles east of Antwerp).

September 27th.—Limburg fell.   Our communications with the Rhine were now shortened, but otherwise there had been little result from the Netherlands campaign during 1703.

October 16th.—Marlborough met the Archduke Charles, who had been proclaimed King of Spain, at Dusseldorf.

December 26th.—Marlborough met the Archduke Charles at Spithead, and escorted him to Windsor.

December 28th.—A detachment of the Allies from Liège and Marke attacked the French in position in the vicinity of Wasseiges.   This raid was completely successful, and raised the *morale* of the Allies.

CHAPTER IV.

1704—General Summary of Events.

Marlborough's plan was to carry the war into the enemy's country and to deal with their field armies.   From the point of view of national resources, the difficulty was that our troops had to be sent to help Portugal, to the West Indies, and to Gibraltar, as well as to Flanders for active operations. Approximately 35,000 men would be required.   Louis XIV made a plan to strike a decisive blow in the Danube Valley. Tallard was to advance from the Rhine, then to join up with Marsin and the Elector of Bavaria and march on Vienna. Vendôme was to co-operate with the main French Army by conquering Louis' enemies in the Tyrol and in Northern Italy.   The Duke of Berwick was to operate in Spain, Villars was to deal with the insurrection in the Cevennes, while Villeroy maintained a defensive attitude in the Netherlands.

Marlborough determined to anticipate the French and to march to the Danube, where he would join Eugène and so would interpose his army between the enemy and Vienna.   He did not inform the Dutch authorities of his plan, as the Dutch could not realize that a victory on the Danube would affect them in the Netherlands.   They could not see that they must defeat an enemy's field army in order to gain conclusive results, and that for this they must disengage the bulk of their forces from the Netherlands and concentrate all available forces on the Danube for a decisive battle with the main French Army. Marlborough let it be known that he was going to co-operate with the commander of our German Allies in Alsace, in order to carry out operations on the River Moselle, and that then he was going to operate towards Paris.

He made careful preparations beforehand by having the route, from Ruremonde via Bonn, Coblentz and Mainz on the Rhine, Ladenburg and Mondelsheim on the Neckar, Geislingen, Ulm and Donauworth, carefully reconnoitred.   Depots at suitable points were established.   Contracts for shoes and supplies were arranged in the cities of the Middle Rhine.   His force consisted of fifty battalions and ninety squadrons.

He marched his force to Coblentz and thence to Mayence, and thus deceived both the French and the Dutch.

Marlborough then marched to the Neckar, where he met

Eugène, who took command of the Allied troops on the Rhine. Louis of Baden accompanied Marlborough in the march to the Danube. These two commanders now on alternate days commanded the forces. That Marlborough was able to gain a decisive victory at Blenheim was a great achievement, with the handicap of a divided command and with the knowledge that every twenty-four hours his plans, decisions, and orders might be reversed. He had to gain his results within a certain time limit, as Prince Louis of Baden was incapable of adequate and effective co-operation.

Prince Louis was nervous, jealous and suspicious, and was unable to make decisions or to take responsibility at critical moments. His presence was as embarrassing and troublesome as that of the Dutch Deputies. With neither was there the loyal and close co-operation, by which, as F.S.R. tell us, the "component parts of any force can develop fully their inherent power."

The Allies reached Elchingen on the Danube via Ebersbach and Geislingen. The Elector of Bavaria garrisoned Elchingen and then advanced to Dillingen.

Marlborough moved in an easterly direction, with the object of crossing the Danube at Donauworth. The Elector of Bavaria took up a position at Schellenberg, where he was defeated, and then he retired to Augsberg. Tallard marched from Alsace with 25,000 men to co-operate with the Elector of Augsberg.

Eugène followed Tallard, and reached Dillingen. Louis of Baden now invested Ingolstadt, while Marlborough returned to the north of the Danube and joined Eugène east of Hochstadt.

On August 11th, the French and Bavarians who were north of the river marched in an easterly direction towards Marlborough's army. On August 13th, the Battle of Blenheim was fought.

Tallard had in Blenheim a garrison of 9,500. Oberglauheim and Lutzingen were also occupied. Marlborough joined forces with Eugène and they marched across the Kessel and reached the French position at seven in the morning. Tallard was surprised, and did not begin to form up his troops and post his artillery until the Allies were deploying for attack. Luckily for Tallard, on the right Eugène was delayed by the difficulties of the ground, and the battle did not commence till an hour after midday.

Cutts then led an infantry attack against Blenheim. This was repulsed. Marlborough then reinforced Cutts with cavalry. Renewed attacks were, however, repulsed. On the right flank, Eugène's attack also failed. Further assaults were now stopped till the cavalry had crossed the River Nebel. While they were trying to do this, the Danish and Prussian Cavalry, under the Prince of Holstein-Becke, at Oberglauheim were being defeated.

It is interesting at this point to note what General Hamley writes on the subject in his " Operations of War " : —

" Marlborough's special gift was detecting blots in the opposing line where the hostile leader had made a blunder in his dispositions, and directing thereon the decisive attack. In the midst of the fight, when officers and men were heated in the *mêlée* and ordinary generals, perplexed by the turmoil, could do little more than push their reinforcements into the fight, his clear, calm vigilance detected a fatal blunder of arrangements, and his ready skill directed a heavy blow on the vulnerable spot. Thus, at Blenheim, the French in position had allowed Marlborough to draw upon his forces deliberately and without molestation, though the difficulties of the ground were such that Prince Eugène's wing of the Allied Army for many hours retarded in coming into line, during which the English General remained exposed to the possible attack of the full force of the enemy. At length the preparations of the Allies were completed, and they began the action, and while the French made good their ground at the villages, Marlborough observed how weak was their cavalry on the grassy plateau between. He then ceased to push the futile attack on Blenheim, and sent cavalry, infantry and guns over the small marshy stream of the Nebel, at the unguarded points, and breaking through the thin line of horsemen, bore all that stood between his troops and the Danube back upon the river."

When Marlborough had rallied the troops on his right flank, he got into touch with Eugène. Cavalry attacks were now renewed against the centre of the French, who, after two charges, were driven back. They then retreated in disorder to the River Danube and to Hochstadt.

Marlborough pursued and took Tallard prisoner. Blenheim was now isolated, owing to the retreat of troops holding the centre of the French line. This town was now again attacked, and captured. Eleven thousand prisoners were taken, and 12,000 French were killed. The Elector and Marsin burnt Oberglauheim and Lutzingen, and then retired by Dillingen and Lauingen, where they burnt the bridges.

c

Marlborough followed them up to the Rhine, then marched into the Moselle Valley and captured Trèves and Taarbach.

Our losses were approximately 12,000, of which 4,500 were killed.   This crushing defeat inflicted on the French and Bavarians saved Germany and Vienna, raised the prestige of the Allies, and lowered the *morale* of Louis XIV's troops; it invigorated the war party in Holland; it raised the enthusiasm of the English nation for the continuance of the war.

1704—Particular Dates.

January 18th.—Marlborough arrived at the Hague to consider a plan of campaign with the States-General for operating with the main army on the Rhine and the Moselle.

April 21st.—Marlborough arrived at the Hague, in order to make the final preparations for his campaign.   These preparations included the posting of Dutch troops as follows:

Overkirk was sent to the Meuse to counter Villeroy; Slangenburg was to operate up to the Moselle; Salisch was to move to Brabant; and the rest of the Dutch Army was to remain in Flanders for the present.

May 2nd.—Marlborough informed the States' Deputies of his plan to march into Germany.

May 4th.—Marlborough left the Hague.

May 5th.—Marlborough arrived at Bedburg.   His force consisted of seventy-three squadrons and fifty-one battalions, of which fourteen were British.

May 10th.—Marlborough inspected Overkirk's troops at Maestricht.

May 16th.—Marlborough started his march to the River Danube via Kuhlseggen, Coblentz, Mainz, Ladenberg, Sinsheim, Gros Heppach, Elchingen, Giengen, Amerdingen, Ebermergen, Donauworth.   Villeroy started to follow Marlborough towards the River Moselle.

May 25th.—Marlborough with his cavalry, who had gone ahead of his infantry and artillery from Kuhlseggen, reached Coblentz and crossed to the right bank of the Rhine.

May 27th.—Infantry and artillery of Marlborough's army reached Coblentz and crossed the Rhine.   Reinforcements from Prussia and Hanover joined Marlborough's army.

May 29th.—Marlborough and his cavalry reached Cassel. Tallard prepared to occupy a position to cover Landau. Villeroy prepared to co-operate with Tallard.

June 1st.—Marlborough and the cavalry crossed the River Neckar at Ladenberg.   His infantry were at Cassel.   Now that Marlborough had eluded the French, he wrote to the States-General to inform them of his intentions and plans.

June 8th.—Marlborough's infantry and artillery reached Heidelburg.   Here a supply of shoes was provided for the troops.

June 10th.—Marlborough crossed the River Neckar again. This time his crossing-place was south of Heilbronn.   He now halted to enable the infantry and artillery to join him.

Marlborough and Prince Eugène met for the first time. Their meeting-place was Mondelsheim.   There was always close co-operation between Marlborough and Eugène throughout this campaign.   This was in marked contrast to the actions of the Dutch and of Prince Louis of Baden.   Opportunities for military success with the Dutch and with Prince Louis were constantly sacrificed either to short-sighted policy or to nervousness.

The following paragraph in this connection from " The Wars of Marlborough," by Taylor, is interesting :

> " If the forces at the disposal of the Allies had been placed under the unfettered control of a military genius of the first order in these campaigns he would have made an end of the exorbitant power of France.   If Marlborough and Eugène had been fortunate enough to wield the political authority of a Frederick or Napoleon, the war would have been conducted with a single eye to the destruction of the enemy.   But under the conditions which in fact prevailed, the opinions of third-rate generals were treated with respect, while unity of purpose and harmony of action were entirely sacrificed to the selfish and short-sighted ambitions of the various members of the vast confederacy."

June 11th.—Marlborough and Eugène reviewed the troops at Gros Heppach.

June 13th.—Prince Louis of Baden joined Marlborough. It was decided that Marlborough and Prince Louis should command the army of the Danube on alternate days, and that Prince Eugène should command the Stolhofen force and should stop the French from reinforcing their Bavarian army.

C2

June 14th.—Marlborough with his cavalry crossed the Geislingen Pass.   The French Marshals Villeroy and Tallard held a conference at Landau.   They were still uncertain as to whether Marlborough meant to march in an easterly direction on Donauworth or to the west into Alsace.

June 22nd.—Marlborough joined Baden's army ten miles north of Ulm.

June 27th.—Marlborough reached Giengen.   Here he was joined by Hanoverian and Hessian troops.   His force was now 200 squadrons, 48 guns, and 96 battalions.   A force of about 36,000 French and 24,000 Bavarians was now between Lauingen and Dillingen on the Danube.   Villeroy had 36,000 men at Strasburg, and Eugène to oppose him had approximately 20,000.

Marlborough wished to attack the Dillingen force before it could be reinforced.   He wished to occupy the Schellenberg Hill, east of Donauworth, in order to cover the passage of the Danube, and to protect his communications to his bases at Nordlingen and Nuremberg.

This hill was occupied by a detachment of 12,500 men sent by the Elector of Bavaria.

July 1st.—Marlborough's army reached the vicinity of Amerdingen.   Marlborough with his cavalry made a personal reconnaissance of the Schellenberg position.   He heard that Tallard, with a force of 40,000 men, was starting to march through the Black Forest to join the Elector of Bavaria.

July 2nd.—Battle of the Schellenberg.   Marlborough's force of approximately 10,500 men reached the River Wernitz about midday.   His troops were then halted for three hours.   During this time, fascines were cut from the neighbouring woods, to enable the troops to cross the stream running east of Donauworth in front of the entrenchments, which ran from the north-east corner of Donauworth round the Schellenberg to the Danube for a distance of two miles, 1,300 yards from the south-east corner of the town.

At 3 p.m., the troops were formed up, and three hours later Marlborough started to assault the enemy's main position on the Schellenberg after an hour's artillery bombardment from the Berg.   His available force consisted of 6,000 infantry in four lines.   These were the forward assaulting troops.   They were followed by eight battalions in reserve, followed by the cavalry.

The advance was carried out in a south-easterly direction from the Berg, the left of the forward lines being on the woods half a mile north-east of Donauworth.

The fascines carried by the assaulters were to fill in the ditch in front of the enemy's entrenchment; unfortunately, the bulk of the forward troops used them to fill up a ravine which was in the line of their advance 200 yards from the objective.

When they reached the ditch under the enemy's trenches, they suffered heavily owing to the delay in trying to cross it. The defenders now tried to drive our troops back with a counter-attack. This our troops successfully repulsed. The assaulters continued to press their attacks on the north-west corner of the Schellenberg, to which place the commander was forced to send all his available troops.

Dismounted cavalry helped in the assault, which was pressed vigorously by the Imperialists at the point where the Schellenberg entrenchments joined up with Donauworth.

After the fighting had been going on for an hour and a half, and had in parts become hand-to-hand, the defence collapsed at the north-west corner of the position, where the trenches were incomplete. The French and Bavarians retreated in disorder to the temporary bridges erected over the Danube south-east of Donauworth.

Marlborough ordered an immediate pursuit to be carried out. Our losses were estimated at 5,000, and the enemy, it was reported, had lost twice that number, as not more than 3,000 reached the Bavarian camp at Dillingen on that night. In addition, the enemy lost fifteen guns and thirteen colours.

July 5th.—The Allies crossed the Danube and camped at Medingen. This march to the Danube of 250 miles from the Meuse had been accomplished in less than six weeks. The strategical situation of the campaign had been changed by this transfer of the main army into Bavaria without any interference by the French.

July 7th.—Marlborough sent a detachment of 4,000 men to bridge the River Lech at Genderkingen.

July 8th.—A further detachment of 6,000 men was sent to join them. The Allied Army camped at Hammer and Genderkingen. A detachment from the Allied Army was sent to Neuberg, which was evacuated by the enemy, who withdrew to Ingolstadt.

The Elector of Bavaria now retired westwards to Augsberg, where he entrenched his position. He asked Villeroy, who was on the Rhine, to send him reinforcements as early as possible, in order to save his country from being overrun by the Allies.

July 10*th.*—The Allies crossed the River Lech and reached Standa and Rirkheim.

July 12*th.*—Marlborough began the siege of Rain.   This caused considerable delay at the important time when the Franco-Bavarian forces were concentrating to oppose the Allies.   This time might have been employed in preventing the junction of 20,000 men under Tallard with the forces of the Elector of Bavaria, which, if successful, would give the enemy the advantage of superior numbers at the decisive point.

July 16*th.*—The garrison of Rain capitulated.   Marlborough's army reached Holtz and Osterhausen.

July 18*th.*—The Allies occupied Kupach and Aiche.

July 22*nd.*—Marlborough captured Friedberg.

July 23*rd.*—Tallard's force reached Villingen, which he started to besiege.   Marlborough and Louis of Baden gave orders for the villages and castles of Bavaria up to Munich to be destroyed, and for the country to be laid waste, in order to force the Elector to break off his alliance with the French.

Eugène, in order to co-operate with Marlborough and to observe Tallard's movements, left Rothwell with sixty squadrons and twenty battalions.

July 24*th.*—Tallard left Villingen and reached Tutlingen.

August 4*th.*—Tallard arrived at Bieberbach on the Schmütter.   The Allies returned to Aiche.

August 5*th.*—The Allies marched to Schrobenhausen.   The Elector of Bavaria marched to join Tallard at Bieberbach.

August 6*th.*—Gibraltar was captured.

August 8*th.*—Eugène reached Hochstadt, twelve miles west of Donauworth.   He rode over to confer with Marlborough and Louis of Baden.   It was decided that Prince Louis should undertake the siege of Ingolstadt with a force of 20,000 Germans.

August 9*th.*—Marlborough marched to Enheim.   He received information that the Bavarians were marching against Eugène's force at Hochstadt.   Prince Louis reached Neuberg *en route* for Ingolstadt.

August 10th.—Marlborough sent twenty-eight squadrons to help Eugène. These were followed by twenty battalions and guns under General Charles Churchill. Eugène retired to the Kessel.

August 11th.—Churchill's force joined Eugène at Münster. Marlborough crossed the Danube with the remainder of his army in two columns at Merxheim and Donauworth. The opposing forces were now of nearly equal fighting value, namely, approximately 53,000 each. The French had the advantage in artillery in having thirty more guns than the Allies, who had sixty.

Tallard had a strong position about three-quarters of a mile west of the River Nebel, with his right on the Danube at Blenheim, which had been put in a state of defence, and his left on wooded hills. The Allies also were well posted, covering Donauworth and their communications to Nuremberg.

August 12th.—The Allied troops rested. Marlborough and Eugène went forward to Dapfheim to make personal reconnaissance of the enemy's position. They decided to attack, as delay would enable Tallard to strengthen his position, and they would have no reinforcements until Louis of Baden was able to return after the fall of Ingolstadt.

August 13th.—Battle of Blenheim. Marlborough's plan was to make his main attack against Blenheim, held by Clerambault with 8,000 infantry and 1,500 dismounted cavalry. Other attacks were to be made against the centre of the enemy's position between Blenheim and Oberglauheim, held by ten squadrons of cavalry supported by nine battalions and ten more squadrons, while Eugène contained the eighteen battalions stationed in front of Lutzingen. Then Marlborough intended to cut off their retreat to Ulm.

Soon after 7 a.m., the Allied Army began to form up on the eastern bank of the River Nebel, and five bridges were constructed over the stream. It was not till 1 p.m. that the assault against Blenheim started, as the right flank had been considerably delayed by the enemy's left-flank troops, and owing to the difficulty of the country.

This main assault was carried out by Lord Cutts. His force was formed into four lines of infantry, with the cavalry on the right flank.

The first assaulters were checked by the defenders' fire, and were then counter-attacked by eight squadrons of French cavalry, who in turn were stopped by Cutts's second line of infantry and then were charged by our cavalry, who pursued them up to Blenheim. Our cavalry were then forced to retire when they came under the close fire of the French defenders. Four battalions composing the third line were then brought forward to the attack.   They reached the enemy's palisades three times, but were unable to carry the French entrenchments.

Marlborough then decided to make his main attack against the centre of the enemy's position and against Oberglauheim while Cutts remained in observation at Blenheim and contained Clerambault's forces there.   It was not, however, till after 5 p.m. that his forces were established on the west bank of the River Nebel.

General Charles Churchill in the centre, with the Danish and Hanoverian squadrons, had heavy fighting, and so had both the Prince of Holstein-Becke with his Hanoverian battalions in the vicinity of Oberglauheim, and Eugène, farther north, in his attacks against Marsin's positions, and also the Prince of Anhalt with eighteen battalions in his attacks on the Elector of Bavaria's troops near Lutzingen.

Marlborough now formed up 8,000 sabres, and successfully charged the French centre.   Eugène, at the head of his infantry, at the same time drove back the Bavarian troops up to Lutzingen.   The whole of the left wing of the Franco-Bavarian Army gave way when their centre had fallen back in front of Marlborough's cavalry charges.

The pursuit was vigorously carried out until dusk by Prussian squadrons directed towards Sonderheim and Hochstadt.   Tallard and his staff were captured.

The 9,500 French troops in Blenheim were now isolated. Their attempts to cut their way out were checked by Churchill's infantry and by the charges of the British cavalry. They had to make an unconditional surrender.

The Allies' casualties were approximately 12,000; the enemy lost nearly 38,000 men, of whom there were 12,000 killed and 11,000 prisoners.   This battle was the first great and complete defeat of the French Army during the reign of Louis XIV.

The Elector of Bavaria and Marsin retreated through the Black Forest and joined Villeroy's army.   They then all withdrew to the vicinity of Strasburg.

August 14th.—The Allies reached a position near Steinheim. Marlborough now intended to advance up the River Moselle and to invade Alsace.   Prince Louis of Baden was to advance towards Saarlouis.   Opposed to Marlborough on the Moselle, it was expected, would be Villars, and that Marsin would be operating in the Valley of the Upper Rhine, and Villeroy's army of 75,000 was to take the offensive in the Netherlands.

August 15th.—The Allies marched to Soflingen.

August 20th.—Prince Louis of Baden joined Marlborough and Eugène at Soflingen.

August 21st.—The Allies marched to Philipsburg, where they were joined by the troops left by Eugène at Stolhofen.

August 22nd.—Prince Louis of Baden now began to besiege Landau. The troops under Marlborough and Eugène withdrew to Weissenburg on the River Lauter.

October 13th.—Marlborough began to advance on Trèves by sending forward a force to Homburg.

October 24th.—Marlborough reached Hemeskeil, fifteen miles from Trèves.

October 25th.—Marlborough reached Trèves and forced the French out of a fort, called St. Martin, in that town.

October 26th.—Marlborough started to fortify Trèves.

November 1st.—A cavalry camp was formed at Consaarbruck, south-west of Trèves, at the junction of the Saar and the Moselle.

November 3rd.—The Prince of Hesse Cassel was sent forward to besiege Trarbach on the Moselle, thirty miles northeast of Trèves.

November 6th.—Marlborough returned to Landau.

November 8th.—Marlborough arrived at Weissenburg.

November 21st.—Marlborough went to Berlin to negotiate for the supply of 8,000 Prussians to serve under Eugène in Italy.

November 25th.—Landau capitulated.

December 25th.—Marlborough returned to London.

December 26th.—In the House of Lords, Marlborough received a complimentary address, in which it was stated that the exorbitant power of France was checked, and that the Empire was freed from a very dangerous enemy.

CHAPTER V.

1705.—General Summary of Events.

Eugene was sent to Italy, where he gained a victory at Turin over Orleans, Marsin and La Feuillade.

Marlborough wished to invade France by the Moselle Valley, but he was prevented by his Allies. He returned to Flanders, where Villeroy was occupying the Meuse fortresses. He forced a way across an unguarded point on the Little Geete River, through a series of works constructed by the enemy between Namur and Antwerp.

He then proposed to cross the River Dyle, but the Dutch commanders thwarted this project, so he moved round by the source of this river to threaten Brussels from the south. By August 16th, he reached Genappe, and on the following day he was at Frischermont, where he gained touch at Waterloo with the enemy, who were defending Brussels. Marlborough was prevented from winning a victory at Waterloo, by the refusal of the Dutch to fight.

Slangenberg, the Dutch commander, was deprived of his command, but little could now be done except to destroy the enemy's lines between the Demer and the Mehaigne before withdrawing the Army into winter quarters.

Owing to the lack of co-operation by the Allies, Marlborough wished to leave the Netherlands to co-operate with Eugène in Northern Italy in defeating Vendôme, and then to invade France from the south. However, the successes gained by Villars on the Upper Rhine frightened the Dutch and caused them to refuse to join in this plan. Similarly, the Prussian, Hanoverian and Danish Governments refused to send troops to Italy. Marlborough had to be content, therefore, to send a detachment of 10,000 men to reinforce Eugène.

1705—Particular Dates.

May 8th.—Marlborough returned to the Army at Maestricht. He now had obtained the consent of the Dutch to his plan of campaign; accordingly he arranged for an interview with Prince Louis of Baden, in order to accelerate his co-operation.

May 21st.—Marlborough met Prince Louis of Baden, who agreed to operate on the River Saar and to secure the lines of Lauterburg and Stolhofen.   Villeroy captured Huy and began to advance on Liège.

May 26th.—The Dutch and English troops were near Trèves. Marlborough joined them at this place.

June 3rd.—Marlborough's force crossed the River Moselle.

June 4th.—Marlborough's force crossed the River Saar at Consaarbruck, and was joined here by small contingents from Hanover, Hesse and Denmark.   The troops from Baden and Prussia had not arrived.

June 5th.—Marlborough's force reached Eft.   Villars's army (55,000 strong) was in position covering Thionville between Sierk and the Forest of Caldaoven.   Marlborough had not sufficient men without the promised troops from Prussia and Baden to attack Villars.

June 17th.—As Marlborough's promised reinforcements did not arrive, he was forced to abandon his offensive plans on the River Moselle and to return to the River Meuse.

June 18th.—Marlborough left troops at Trèves and Saarbruck, and marched back to Consaarbruck.   Villars sent a detachment to join Villeroy.

June 25th.—Marlborough reached Duren.   Villeroy withdrew from Liège to Tongres.

July 2nd.—Marlborough's and Overkirk's Dutch forces united at Haneff.   Villeroy's army, 70,000 strong, retired behind his fortified lines, which were now complete, and ran from east of Namur to Antwerp via the Mehaigne, the Little Geete and the Great Geete.

July 4th.—Marlborough's force arrived at Lens-les-Béguines. He decided to force the French lines by demonstrating with the Dutch troops towards their southern extremity while he crossed with his main force near Elixem and Neerhespen.   He detached a small force to Huy.   Overkirk reached St. Servais.

July 11th.—Huy was taken by the Allies.

July 17th.—Overkirk crossed the Mehaigne and concentrated opposite the French lines between Meffle and Namur.   Villeroy marched 40,000 men towards Merdrop to deal with this feint. Marlborough recalled the detachment from Huy.

July 18th.—By 4 a.m., Marlborough's advance guard of twenty-two battalions and twenty squadrons were within a mile of the French lines at Wanghe, having made a night march of fifteen miles.   Pontoons were laid for the cavalry, and the infantry scrambled across.   The French were completely surprised.   At the points of attack—namely, at Neershespen, Wanghe and Elixem—there were only three battalions and two squadrons behind their forward piquets, which were quickly driven back.

The Allies' advance guard was supported by the cavalry of the main body in time to press forward in pursuit of the retreating Bavarians.   The Elector, however, brought up reinforcements of fifty squadrons and twenty battalions to the south-west of Elixem.   These were now charged by Marlborough, leading his cavalry.

The enemy at first gave way, but later were able to rally and counter-attack.

Marlborough's second cavalry charge, however, routed them. Villeroy and the Elector, seeing this, ordered a withdrawal in a westerly direction towards Louvain.   The Great Geete was crossed near Judoigne and, covered by two Bavarian infantry brigades, reached their appointed destination at the Parc Camp, protected by the guns in Louvain.   Marlborough was forced to halt, as his troops were very tired after the fight and the long night march.

Overkirk's Dutch army had joined the main army after the battle, and so Marlborough was anxious to press forward with these troops, in order to get the full results from his success, but the Dutch generals refused to pursue.   The Allies remained that night encamped between Rosbeek and Tirlemont.

Marlborough had, at the cost of a few casualties, inflicted several thousand casualties on the enemy, and had broken through the lines which it was thought were impassable.   His plan was well conceived and boldly carried out.   That he was not able to turn his success to an immediate and striking victory was most disappointing.

July 19th.—The Allies advanced towards the Dyle, which had become impassable owing to heavy rain.   On the western bank of this river, Villeroy's army was in position in the vicinity of Louvain.   Marlborough had, during the day, struck the rearguard of the retreating French Army, and had taken 1,500 prisoners.

The Dutch were most reluctant to attempt to force the passage of the River Dyle.

July 29th.—Marlborough attempted to cross the River Dyle. A British detachment crossed at Corbeek Dyle, and a Dutch detachment crossed at Neeryssche.

The French had again been surprised, and there was nothing now to be done except for the main body of the Allies to press on resolutely. This the Dutch refused to do, and even their advanced detachment was recalled. Marlborough had to abandon this operation.

In view of French reinforcements being sent up to Villeroy owing to the inaction of Prince Louis of Baden in Alsace, Marlborough decided to move to Genappe and then to wheel in a northerly direction.

August 15th.—Marlborough marched to Corbais. Overkirk marched to Nil St. Martin.

August 16th.—The Allies reached Genappe.

August 17th.—The Allies began to wheel to the north, and reached the line La Hulpe-Braine l'Alleud. General Charles Churchill, with twenty squadrons and twenty battalions, was sent to the Soignies Forest to turn the French flank.

Villeroy was behind the River Yssche, with the Soignies Forest on his right flank.

August 18th.—The Allies crossed the River Lasne. Marlborough reconnoitred the enemy's position, and decided to cross the Yssche at Overyssche.

August 19th.—Owing to delays on the march in the Dutch columns, and owing to their guns being behind their baggage, Marlborough had not been able to form up for attack till noon. Even then, although Overkirk had previously promised to co-operate, the Dutch commanders delayed in making up their minds to attack, and finally decided that the French position was too strong to be attacked.

Reinforcements by this time had reached the French at the point where Marlborough intended to assault, and he was obliged to withdraw in an easterly direction.

The troops now went into winter quarters, after destroying the enemy's lines between Demer and Mehaigne, and Marlborough went to the Hague to confer with the States-General.

November 1st.—Marlborough arrived at Vienna, where he was able to improve the relations between the Emperor and Frederick of Prussia.

November 30th.—Marlborough was at Berlin. The Prussian, Hanoverian and Danish Governments refused to sanction the employment of their troops in Italy, and the Dutch would not allow their Army to leave the Netherlands. Marlborough could, therefore, only help Eugène in Italy by sending him 10,000 men.

CHAPTER VI.

1706.—General Summary of Events.

Marlborough wished to transfer his army to Italy to co-operate with Eugène. He was, however, persuaded by the Dutch to remain in Flanders, as Marshal Villars surprised Prince Louis of Baden in his lines on the Mottar, and captured the two magazines. This frightened the Dutch, and made them very anxious to keep Marlborough. Accordingly they agreed that their Deputies in future would accept his orders instead of issuing them, if the Duke would consent to make his main theatre of war in Flanders. To this Marlborough had to agree.

The over-confidence of Villeroy soon gave him another opportunity of distinguishing himself. The French Army was in an entrenched position behind the River Dyle. Villeroy determined to leave these entrenchments and to attack the Allies before they were joined by the Danes, Prussians and Hanoverians.

On May 19th, 1706, accordingly, he began his advance towards Tirlemont on the Great Geete. Marlborough, who was at Maestricht, with the Dutch and the British forces on the Upper Demer at Bilsen, began to march in a southerly direction towards Borcloen. Villeroy at this time crossed the Great Geete and marched towards Judoigne. By Sunday morning, May 23rd, the opposing forces, each approximately 60,000 strong, were close together. Villeroy's army was between the Tomb of Ottomond, which is at the summit of the plain and the village of Autréglise.

Close to the sources of the Little Geete is Ramillies, behind which the ground rises and forms an undulating plain, which is the highest ground in Brabant.

From the highest point in this Plain of St. André, when the morning mist had cleared, Villeroy could see the approaching columns. He formed up his army in two lines facing east. The position chosen was a strong one, as on his centre and left was the Little Geete.

Taviers, on the River Mehaigne, on his right flank, was protected by swampy ground bordering the river. Where the Little Geete rose about the centre of the position, the ground

30

was swampy.   The most suitable ground, therefore, for the movement of troops was on the French right between the village of Ramillies at the Little Geete sources and Taviers.

Marlborough realized this in his preliminary reconnaissance with Overkirk.   He saw that the concave position of the French militated against rapidity of movement to reinforce the flanks of their position, and that, though the French left was in a strong position, the marshy ground and the Little Geete in their front would limit the mobility of their cavalry in this area, and would prevent them from carrying out the cavalry rôle of harassing the Allies' northern flank.   He recognized that the capture of the Tomb of Ottomond would enable him to dominate and turn the whole position from the south.

He therefore decided that he would mystify and mislead the French as to the direction of his attack, by making a feint on their left flank while he struck with all available force at the decisive place, that is, on to the ridge between Taviers and Ramillies, and then towards the Tomb of Ottomond.

After an artillery duel, four Dutch battalions advanced on the southern flank and captured Francqnée and advanced on Taviers.   At the same time, Marlborough made a demonstration against Autréglise, and with twelve battalions attacked Ramillies.

Overkirk's cavalry advanced slowly on the left flank, and, as soon as Taviers was captured, charged successfully through the first French line.   The French line on the ridge checked the Dutch until Marlborough, at the head of fresh squadrons, rallied them, and then continued the attack, helped by twenty fresh squadrons and by Danish horse.

At Ramillies, the French resisted until the Danish cavalry had pushed forward to the Tomb of Ottomond.   The rest of the cavalry west of Taviers routed the French between this village and the river.

Once the Tomb of Ottomond—which commanded the whole plain—was captured, the French positions became untenable. Ramillies was carried at 6.30 p.m., and the French lines south of it gave way.   Villeroy tried to bring his cavalry from the left flank to stem the rout, but they were not in time.

The French cavalry of the right wing was driven from the field and their infantry on this wing was demoralized by the assaults of the Allies' cavalry and infantry.

Marlborough now ordered the whole of the infantry, supported by two cavalry regiments on his northern flank, to advance on Offus and Autréglise.

The French left flank was now turned, and their whole line broke and withdrew in panic towards Judoigne, abandoning their baggage and most of their guns.   Marlborough and Overkirk pressed on in pursuit beyond Judoigne till, at 2 a.m., the troops had covered fifteen miles from the battlefield, and were six miles from Louvain.   Orkney, with the British cavalry, continued the pursuit up to the gates of Louvain.

On the following day, the passage of the River Dyle and the town of Louvain were in the Allies' possession.   The French entire losses were computed to be 15,000 men, 50 guns and 80 standards.   The Allies had 1,000 killed and 2,500 wounded.

The consequences of this battle were that the French evacuated Brussels, Malines and Lierre.   Villeroy could no longer hold the line of the River Scheldt.   Ghent, Bruges, Antwerp and Ostend surrendered.   Menin, Dendermond and Ath were also captured, and the French fell back to their own frontier.

1706.—PARTICULAR DATES.

April 25th.—Marlborough arrived at the Hague in order to co-ordinate a plan of campaign with the Dutch, Prussians and Hanoverians.   The difficulty of this was that the Germans wanted to operate on the Moselle, the Dutch wished to fight in Flanders, and Marlborough wanted to transfer his forces to the Plains of Lombardy.

May 1st.—The decision of the Allies was influenced by the action of Marshal Villars, who took the offensive against Prince Louis of Baden commanding 7,000 men on the River Mottar.   Prince Louis was surprised and driven back across the Rhine.   The Allies then decided to carry on a campaign in Flanders.

May 9th.—Marlborough concentrated the Dutch troops at Tongres and the British troops at Borcloen.

May 19th.—The Dutch and British were concentrated in the vicinity of Bilsen on the Upper Demer.   Marlborough's army now was 130 squadrons, seventy-five battalions, and ninety pieces of artillery.

May 20th.—The Allies moved south to Borcloen.   Marlborough intended now to strike at Namur, in the hope that this move would cause Villeroy to leave his entrenched positions and fight a battle in the open.

May 22nd.—The Danish contingent, under the Duke of Wirtemberg, arrived.   They had been waiting for their arrears of pay.   Marlborough's army was now of practically equal strength to that of the French.

On this day, news was brought in that Villeroy and the Elector of Bavaria, with an army of 130 squadrons, seventy-six battalions, and seventy-four pieces of artillery, had crossed the Great Geete, and was moving on Judoigne.

May 23rd.—At 4 a.m., the Allies began to march towards Ramillies in eight columns, reaching Merdrop about 8 a.m.

The French were then in the plain west of Ramillies. By 10 a.m., the opposing armies were making dispositions for battle. The French had the bulk of their cavalry between Taviers and Ramillies, with a detachment of five battalions in Francqnée. Two lines of infantry covered the ground between Ramillies and Offus. On their left flank, between Offus and Autréglise, the infantry were supported by cavalry.

Marlborough's lines were similarly formed up. On his right, east of the Little Geete and of Offus and Autréglise, were the British infantry under Orkney, supported by British cavalry under Lumley.

Dutch infantry formed the first line in the centre, supported by British infantry lines. On the left, between Ramillies and Taviers, were the Dutch under Overkirk, supported by the Danes. Four Dutch battalions faced Francqnée.

1 p.m. The Allies began their advance. On the right flank, Marlborough made a feint. He advanced the British line towards Autréglise and Offus. This shook Villeroy's confidence, and he began to conform to the movements of the Allies. He reinforced his left from his centre.

Marlborough withdrew his first line, after it had advanced across the Little Geete, to support the left centre of his position. The original second line became the first line, and contained the French on their left flank.

1.30 p.m. The artillery duel began. The Dutch detachment of four battalions captured Francqnée. The French reinforcements sent forward to retake it were driven back by Overkirk's cavalry. The Danes and Dutch then fought their way forward along the River Mehaigne.

2.30 p.m. Twelve Allied battalions assaulted Ramillies with cavalry, attacking in four lines. The first lines of the French cavalry were routed. Their second line checked the advance of the Allies, who in turn were then charged by French cavalry and driven back.

Here Marlborough personally rallied the troops until reinforcements were brought from the right flank.

D

5 p.m.   The fighting spread northwards again.   British infantry and cavalry crossed the Geete, and advanced on Autréglise and Offus, and drove back the Bavarian Guards and French troops in this area.

By this time, the Danes and Dutch had got to a position along the Mehaigne behind the French right flank.   The whole French position then became untenable, when the Allies' cavalry and infantry reinforced the centre and drove the French from Ramillies and from the ridge south of it.

The pursuit was vigorously carried out till 2 a.m. by the British cavalry for fifteen miles.   The French could not retire in a south-westerly direction towards Charleroi, as Danish cavalry were on their southern flank.   They had to withdraw towards Brussels.

May 24th.—3 a.m.   The pursuit was continued towards Louvain.   The Allies' main body reached Meldert.

May 25th.—The main body crossed the River Dyle at Louvain.

May 26th.—Marlborough's army arrived at Dieghem, north of Brussels.

May 27th.—Marlborough crossed the Senne at Vilvorde, and reached Grimberghen.

May 28th.—The French continued to retreat to Ghent.

May 30th.—The Scheldt was bridged at Gavre.   Ghent and Bruges capitulated.

June 2nd.—The garrison of Oudenarde surrendered. Antwerp was now isolated.

June 17th.—Antwerp garrison surrendered.   The siege of Ostend was begun under Overkirk.

Marlborough endeavoured to get Prince Louis of Baden to take the offensive on the Upper Rhine, where he outnumbered his opponents.   Such action would relieve the pressure against the Duke of Savoy, whom Eugène was helping.

Marlborough was offered the Governorship of the Spanish Netherlands.   This offer was later refused.

June 19th.—Marlborough with his army, less the detachments at Ostend, on the Charente and at Dendermond, was at Roulers.

June 24th.—An attack was made by the Allies on Dendermond.

June 28th.—Marlborough moved to Rousselaer.

July 5th.—An attack was made by the Allies on Ostend.

July 6th.—Ostend capitulated, and so a new line of communication with England was opened.   Marlborough's army camped between Courtrai and Harlebeke.

July 23rd.—The siege of Menin was begun.

August 22nd.—Menin surrendered.

August 29th.—Dendermond was besieged.

September 5th.—The garrison of Dendermond capitulated.

September 16th.—Overkirk invested Ath.   Marlborough withdrew across the River Scheldt.

October 10th.—The garrison of Ath surrendered.   Vendôme, commanding a French army, was at Valenciennes.   He was superseded by Villeroy, who brought up reinforcements, available owing to Prince Louis of Baden not engaging them on the Upper Rhine.

November.—Owing to bad weather, no further operations were possible during this year.   The troops went into winter quarters; the captured fortresses being garrisoned and made defensible.

CHAPTER VII.

1707.—General Summary of Events.

There were no important operations in Flanders. The English were defeated at Almanza, in Spain, and the Germans were defeated at Stolhofen. These defeats caused the Dutch to distrust Marlborough and to thwart his operations.

The Emperor, by concluding a treaty with France for the neutrality of Italy, enabled the French to concentrate superior forces against Marlborough in the field. Prince Louis of Baden died, and was replaced on the Rhine by the Margrave of Baireuth, who was equally inactive and unenterprising.

The French commander in Alsace was able to drive Baireuth's troops from the Stolhofen lines, and then to over-run Franconia. This was a year of disappointment. The Elector of Hanover (afterwards George I) replaced the Margrave. The situation on the Rhine had to be re-established by diverting to this area Saxon troops who were to have fought in Marlborough's campaign in Flanders.

The Dutch vetoed Marlborough's plans for operating on the River Moselle. Also his diversion against Toulon by land and sea came to nothing.

The French, under Vendôme, were content to be on the defensive. Marlborough, however, twice nearly surprised them in Flanders. They just escaped in time. The Emperor made a movement towards Provence, but so late in the year that, when Marlborough was able to move, bad weather prevented him from carrying out any successful operations, as the Dutch Deputies prevented him from taking action on the one occasion when he did have the opportunity of striking a decisive blow.

In the course of this year, Marlborough visited Charles XII of Sweden, after his victories at Narva, Riga and Klissow, at Dresden. Louis XIV was hopeful of getting him as an ally of France. Marlborough, however, managed to divert him from Germany to Russia, where he was, two years later, ruined at Pultowa. When Marlborough returned to England in November, he found that there was discontent in the Cabinet at the prolongation of the war, and owing to the defeat at Almanza.

However, the Whig majority in Parliament voted the usual supplies; and, in addition to budget, included ten thousand more men for the Army.

1707—PARTICULAR DATES.

January 4th.—Prince Louis of Baden died and was succeeded by the Margrave of Baireuth.

April 6th.—Marlborough landed in Holland.

April 20th.—Marlborough left the Hague in order to visit Charles XII and to prevent him from joining the French cause.

April 25th.—Galway's army was defeated by the Duke of Berwick, commanding the Franco-Spanish Army at Almanza. Owing to this defeat, the province of Valencia was lost.

April 27th.—Marlborough reached Alt Ränstadt, where he had an interview with Charles XII.   He gained a diplomatic triumph.   Charles XII decided not to enter into any agreement with Louis XIV.

April 30th.—Marlborough began his return journey to Holland.

May 2nd. — Marlborough successfully negotiated with Augustus II for a contingent of 4,500 Saxons to co-operate with the Allies.

May 5th.—Marlborough visited King Frederick of Prussia, and smoothed down the troubles caused by the intrigues at his court.

May 8th.—Marlborough returned to the Hague.

May 15th.—Marlborough concentrated 164 squadrons, 97 battalions, and 112 guns at Anderlecht, near Brussels.

May 21st.—Marlborough moved his army to Bellinghen and Lembecq.   The French, under Vendôme, assembled approximately 100,000 men in the vicinity of Mons.   Vendôme's instructions were not to fight at a disadvantage.

May 26th.—Marlborough's army reached the vicinity of Soignies.   Vendôme advanced towards Sombreffe.

May 28th.—Marlborough advanced to the vicinity of Hal. The French moved towards Louvain.

May 30th.—Marlborough marched towards Terbank.   The Dutch Deputies vetoed any further offensive action.

June 1st.—Marlborough occupied a position at Meldert to oppose the French at Gembloux and to cover the approaches into Brabant between the River Dyle and the Geete.

June 30th.—The opposing armies remained in these positions for two months.   The Allied Army under Eugène began its advance on Toulon, by crossing the River Var.

July 15th.—Eugène's army and a British fleet were in the vicinity of Toulon.   Vendôme and Villars were accordingly ordered to send detachments to the south.

August 10th.—Marlborough then decided to profit by this weakening of forces in his front, and to march southward. His army crossed the River Dyle at Florival.

August 11th.—Marlborough marched to Nivelles.

August 12th.—Marlborough sent forward a detachment under Tilly to engage Vendôme's rearguard. Owing to delays caused by the state of the roads and by the rain, this detachment was not able to carry out its mission.

August 14th.—The Allies were in the vicinity of Soignies. The French had hurriedly withdrawn to Chievres, having lost 2,000 stragglers in their retreat.   Bad weather caused Marlborough to halt.

August 31st.—The weather improved, and Marlborough was able to advance.   Eugène had not sufficient numbers to invest Toulon and also to deal with the detachments arriving from Spain after the Franco-Spanish victory at Almanza.   He had to withdraw behind the Var.

September 1st.—The Allies crossed the Dendre at Ath, and, by threatening the left flank of the French, caused them to retreat towards the Scheldt, in order to avoid battle.

September 5th. — The Allies crossed the Scheldt at Oudenarde.

September 7th.—The Allies reached Rolleghan and Helchin. Vendôme withdrew behind the Marque towards Lille.

September 14th.—Marlborough sent a detachment to forage the country up to Tournai, in order to induce the French to leave their positions covered by the guns of Lille.   Vendôme, however, avoided an action at all costs.

October.—Both armies went into winter quarters.

November 18th.—Marlborough returned to England.

CHAPTER VIII.

1708.—General Summary of Events.

In the early part of the year, there was manœuvring by both Marlborough and Vendôme. Marlborough did not wish to take the offensive until Prince Eugène joined him from the Moselle. The German powers delayed Eugène from joining him with the army of the Moselle. The plan agreed upon by these two commanders was that they should unite as early as possible and attack before the French could draw in all their detachments in Flanders.

The French Army (100,000 strong) in Flanders was commanded by Vendôme, who suddenly made himself master of Ghent and Bruges and of the navigation of the River Scheldt and the River Lys.

Marlborough, with an army of 80,000 men, started to attack him, but he withdrew behind the River Dendre and then marched on Oudenarde. Marlborough ordered this town to be occupied by Lord Chandos's troops from Ath before the French could reach it. Vendôme then invested Oudenarde, and posted a covering force at Lessines on the River Dendre.

Eugène arrived ahead of his army and joined Marlborough. This was fortunate, as Marlborough was suffering from fever brought on by worries with his Allies, and Eugène's presence relieved him of much of his anxiety.

The two commanders decided to attack the enemy north of Oudenarde, but not by a direct assault. Their plan was to interpose troops between the hostile army and the French frontier, and to compel Vendôme to fight facing Paris and with his back to Antwerp. Accordingly, the Allies marched rapidly to the River Dendre, which was bridged. They then crossed at Herfelingen. Vendôme then retreated across the River Scheldt at Gavre. Marlborough followed up the French Army.

General Cadogan, commanding the forward troops consisting of eight squadrons and sixteen battalions, with pontoons and thirty-two guns, reached the River Scheldt on July 11th, after a fifteen-mile march. He constructed pontoon bridges over the river, and the whole British Army was able to cross later.

By 2 p.m. on this day (July 11th), Marlborough's army of 80,000 men had covered fifty miles, including the passage of two rivers, in forty-eight hours, before starting the Battle of Oudenarde.

Marlborough, by this marching feat, outmanœuvred the French. The first French objective had been Gavre, on the Scheldt, in order to check the advance of the Allies on Bruges. Marlborough's advance guard under Cadogan reached Eyne, on the River Scheldt, six miles west of Gavre, after a fifteen-mile march.

Soon after Cadogan had reached his position, Vendôme's advance guard, under Biron, unconscious of his presence, began to march across his front. Cadogan's available squadrons were at once sent forward to attack.

The battle soon after this became general, as troops came up on either side.

Vendôme took up a position parallel to the river as quickly as he could from north-west of Eyne towards Asper, with his left flank north of the River Norken, the remainder of his troops between this river and the River Scheldt from Heurne on the left via Bevere towards Mooreghem on the right.

These faulty dispositions, with the weakness of having part of their forces separated from the main position by a river, were due to divided counsels. The Duke of Brunswick wished to post the whole of the French Army north of the River Norken between Asper and Wanneghem on the Huysse Heights. The result was that some obeyed his orders, and others carried out Vendôme's original commands.

The French on the left bank of the river had a good defensive position north of Oudenarde, protected by rolling downs called " couters." Of these, the Boser Couter on their right flank could have been made into a strong position.

Three Allied battalions crossed close to Eyne, while the Hanoverian cavalry moved up in rear of this village. Seven battalions, preceded by thirty squadrons, on the French right flank had marched down towards Eyne. These seven battalions, being left at Eyne, became isolated and were severely dealt with by the Allied infantry, three being captured and four were cut up, and the French cavalry arriving to support them was charged by the Hanoverian Horse and driven north.

The Duke of Burgundy now took the offensive and advanced south of the River Norken with some of his troops towards Bevere and Groenewald. Marlborough reinforced the troops between Heurne, Bevere and Eyne with all available troops north of the River Scheldt.

As the troops crossed, they were sent up to reinforce regiments who were holding their positions covering the crossings. Two of Cadogan's advanced regiments which had been sent up to Groenewald were in a dangerous position, as they were opposed by thirty French battalions, and these were the first to be reinforced.

At first, twenty battalions crossed the river and came up on their left and outflanked the French, who in turn brought up more troops to extend the line of the fighting farther southwest to Schaerken. Then Marlborough handed over the command of the right wing, which was brought up to a strength of sixty battalions, to Eugène.

Marlborough on the left wing had available twenty battalions composed of Dutch, Hanoverians and Prussians. With these he gradually forced the French right flank back to Diepenbeek, and then he launched against this open flank the rest of his reserves of cavalry and infantry which Overkirk took round under cover of the Boser Couter to attack the right rear of the French position.

The French right flank was now assailed from the south, the west, and the north. Their cavalry in this part of the field tried to make a stand, but without success. Eugène helped Cadogan to regain lost ground, and was able to drive back and pass through the French first lines, and to enable the Prussian cavalry to charge their second line. This charge, however, was met by French Household Cavalry, and was repulsed. The French still had some reserves who had not yet been in action. These were the battalions on the French left which had been posted north of the River Norken by Burgundy. It was, however, too late to use them to restore the battle. The French infantry was too much shaken.

Marlborough had decisively defeated their right wing; Eugène was driving them back on the remainder of the front. In addition, the French reserve battalions north of the river were so placed that, owing to the marshy ground in their front, they could not rapidly advance.

The British cavalry was placed on Eugène's right ready to charge down on the French cavalry if they advanced against Eugène's eastern flank, which was consequently secured. Eugène was able to press forward in this area round the French left flank while Marlborough had completely enveloped their other flank. Light was now beginning to fail, and it was difficult in the fighting in this close country to distinguish friend from enemy. Darkness saved the French Army from destruction or capture.

Burgundy gave the order for retreat towards Ghent, and the French Army escaped during the night and next day in complete disorder.   The French were now demoralized.   Our losses were just over 3,000; those of the French were more than twice as many.   In addition, they lost some 9,000 prisoners and 2,000 deserters, 10 guns and 95 standards.

Early on the following morning, forty squadrons were sent in pursuit of the French Army.   These were followed later by thirty-four battalions.   Eugène returned to his own army—about 30,000 strong—which he brought up from Alsace. Berwick, however, had observed this movement, and followed them up with the greater part of his army.

Vendôme's army, with Berwick's reinforcement, was now 100,000 strong, and took up a position in a strongly fortified camp behind the Bruges-Ghent Canal in the vicinity of Ghent. Marlborough's plan now was to advance towards Paris.   This, however, was judged to be impracticable by the Dutch and by Eugène unless Lille was first captured.

The siege of Lille was, therefore, undertaken instead.   Lille was strongly fortified, under the direction of Vauban, and within its citadel was a very strong point.   Marshal Boufflers, commanding 15,000 men, held Liège.   Vendôme, with an army of 100,000 men, was in a strong position, covered by the Canal of Bruges.   Marlborough's army was 84,000 strong. Vendôme interrupted Marlborough's communications by water and compelled the Allies to bring their siege materials by land from Brussels.

Eugène, however, was able to escort the siege train safely to Lille without any loss, although the French had 80,000 men on the flank of his convoy, which was fifteen miles long.   On both sides raids were made; by the French into Belgium, and by the Allies into Artois.

The conduct of the siege of Lille was entrusted to Eugène with 40,000 men.   Marlborough commanded the covering army of 60,000 men at Helchin.   On both sides, on August 24th, the artillery bombardment began.

On August 31st, Vendôme and Berwick advanced to raise the siege.   Marlborough, although his numbers were 30,000 less than the French, advanced to meet them.

The French commanders did not continue to carry out their plans at once, as they were jealous of each other, and they were afraid of Marlborough.   The result was that, when orders came from French Headquarters at Versailles sanctioning an advance, their opportunity for successful action had passed.   Marlborough's entrenched position was too strong to be attacked.

The French then retired towards Oudenarde.

Marlborough wished to follow them up, but the Dutch Deputies refused to allow this operation. The siege progressed slowly. By September 5th, two breaches were made, but our attempt to gain a footing in the position led to a loss of 2,600 men. All lines of approach to Lille, except one, were in the enemy's possession.

On September 20th, Eugène led an assault, reinforced by 5,000 British troops. This was unsuccessful, only a small part of the enemy's works being captured. Eugène was wounded, and 3,000 of our men were put out of action.

Marlborough now took command of the siege operations and of the covering army. He ordered a fresh assault to be made on September 23rd. The troops effected a lodgment in the enemy's works. Vendôme and Berwick now occupied strong positions along the River Scarpe and the River Scheldt between Douai and Ghent, in order to prevent convoys from Brussels reaching the Allies.

Here our command of the sea was of great value. Ostend was in our hands, and was organized as a new base, where supplies were landed.

In order to ensure the safety of the first convoy of 700 wagons, Marlborough sent twelve battalions and 1,500 sabres to Ostend, twelve battalions to Thourout, and eighteen squadrons, under Cadogan, to Roulers. Vendôme sent de la Motte, with 20,000 men, to Wynendale, to intercept the convoy. The French encountered our cavalry at Ichtegem.

Warning was at once sent to General Webb, commanding the Thourout detachment. This General then collected all available troops in the vicinity—approximately twenty battalions and a squadron of cavalry—and marched towards Ichtegem, where he took up a position in three lines covering the Wynendale defile, with his flanks protected by woods in each of which he concealed a battalion.

The French bombarded Webb's position for nearly two hours without much effect, and then attacked with four lines of infantry supported by four lines of cavalry. When they approached the position, they were completely surprised by the fire from the German battalions in the woods on both flanks.

The French at first gained a footing in Webb's forward lines, but pressure was maintained against their flank and front, the gaps in our lines were closed, and their losses became so heavy that they broke in confusion and withdrew, having lost nearly 4,000 and all their artillery in two hours.

During this action, the convoy safely continued its journey from Ostend, and reached the Allies' lines on September 30th.

Vendôme now tried to cut off the Allies' communication with Ostend, by opening the dykes and flooding the country.

Marlborough had then to convoy his supplies in flat-bottomed boats and in high-wheeled vehicles. On October 22nd, Boufflers retired to the citadel of Lille, where he continued to hold out.

While the citadel was being besieged, the Elector of Hanover brought a force from the Rhine and began to besiege Brussels. Marlborough made a night march on November 26th, crossed the Scheldt in two places, surprised the French troops, and took a thousand prisoners. He then sent back the bulk of his troops to continue the siege of Lille under Eugène, and took a detachment of two battalions and some cavalry to Alost. The Elector, hearing of this, hurriedly left Brussels. Lille fell on December 9th.

By a vigorous movement, Marlborough regained Ghent. Bruges also capitulated, and the navigation of the River Scheldt and of the River Lys was regained. Marlborough and Eugène then sent their troops into winter quarters on the Flemish frontier.

1708.—PARTICULAR DATES.

April 9th.—Marlborough sailed for the Hague and met Eugène there. They decided to co-operate in Flanders. This was necessary, as Marlborough had an inferiority in numbers by twelve battalions and nineteen squadrons to Vendôme's army. In order, however, to mislead the French as to their real intentions, Eugène's army was left on the Moselle. The French accordingly sent to oppose it a considerable detachment, under Berwick and the Elector of Bavaria.

May 21st.—Marlborough assembled his army at Anderlecht.

May 26th.—The French marched to Soignies from Mons. Eugène's army was ordered to concentrate near Coblentz.

June 1st.—The French marched to the line Genappe-Braine l'Alleud.

June 3rd.—Marlborough marched to Parc, five miles southeast of Louvain. The French halted at Gembloux. In spite of their numerical superiority, they would not take the offensive.

July 3rd.—The French marched westwards from Braine l'Alleud towards Grammont, sending detachments to surprise and capture Ghent and Bruges. The citizens of these towns were not satisfied with the Dutch administration. French money and promises increased their disaffection, and paved the way for their surrender to Vendôme.

July 5th.—Bruges surrendered.   Marlborough marched towards Anderlecht and Tourbeck in two columns, covered by a cavalry brigade advancing on Alost, following up the French Army, whose rearguard and baggage were captured.

July 6th.—Marlborough moved to Assche, in order to protect Brussels and to prevent a panic among the inhabitants. Eugène rode ahead of his cavalry, and joined Marlborough at Assche.   His presence was most welcome.   He was able to relieve the strain on Marlborough, who was suffering from fever.

July 7th.—Ghent capitulated.   Vendôme began to march towards Oudenarde, and ordered up siege guns from Tournai to this place.

July 8th.—Marlborough sent forward an advance party of 700 men and a cavalry regiment to Oudenarde.

July 9th.—The Allies moved in a south-easterly direction to Herfelingen.   Before the next morning, Lessines had been occupied by nine squadrons and eight battalions.

July 10th.—The Allies' main body reached Lessines.   This march had been accomplished in less than thirty-six hours.   It was a considerable feat of endurance, and it accomplished its object in surprising and outmarching the French, who, finding that Lessines was occupied, marched to a position on the Scheldt, in order to cover Ghent and Bruges.

July 11th.—Battle of Oudenarde was fought.

Marlborough sent forward his advance guard of eight squadrons and sixteen battalions, with pontoons and thirty-two guns, under Cadogan, to secure the passage of the River Scheldt at Oudenarde.   By 2 p.m., Cadogan was crossing the river, and was able to send his cavalry to charge and drive back the French cavalry advancing from Gavre.   The French commanders each wished to carry out a different plan. Vendôme wanted to attack the Allies as they crossed the River Scheldt between Heurne and the road leading to Mooreghem. The Duke of Burgundy wanted to take up a position on the high ground north of the River Norken.   Vendôme sent forward seven battalions, preceded by thirty squadrons of cavalry, to cover the forming up of his troops.   The battalions went forward as far as Eyne, where they were isolated from the rest of the French Army.

Cadogan was able to deal decisively with these troops.

By 3 p.m., Marlborough had some of his cavalry at Bevere and the remainder of his army was in the vicinity of the Scheldt bridges near Oudenarde.

4 p.m.   The first battalions of the Allies' main body to cross the river were sent up to Groenewald.   These had to withstand the attacks of thirty French battalions—who had crossed at Gavre—until Marlborough was able to reinforce them with twenty more battalions as they became available north of the river.   The line gradually extended to the west, with the fighting being carried out at close range in the enclosed country until the line of combatants was extended up to Schaerken.   The French gained some ground in the centre and between Bevere and Mooreghem.

6 p.m.   Reinforcements of infantry coming up were ordered by Marlborough to the right flank.   The French in this part of the field were gradually driven back to Diepenbeek.

Eugène was now given command of the right wing, and, with all available men, pushed the French back to Groenewald.

The Prussian cavalry exploited this success by a charge up to Royeghem, 2,000 yards north of Groenewald and the forward Prussian line.   Here they were checked by French reserves posted behind the hedges, and they were driven back by French Household Cavalry.

The British cavalry were kept by Eugène as a final reserve to be used as required and to be available to attack the French troops north of the River Norken if they should come into action.

Now that the enemy were pressed back on their left centre and were held on the rest of the front, Marlborough decided to seize the Boser Couter.   This hill dominated the whole of the French right flank and by advancing on its western side, troops would have a covered approach round to the rear of the French if it was unoccupied.   The French had neglected to put any troops on this vantage-point, which, if in our possession, would make their position untenable.

Overkirk was ordered to occupy the Boser Couter with all the available cavalry and infantry not actually engaged under Marlborough in driving the French north of Bevere.

This order was easily and quickly carried out, as there was no opposition by the French.

8.30 p.m.   As soon as Overkirk was on the hill, he changed direction to the east on to the French right rear.

The French in this flank were completely surprised when the Prince of Orange and Tilly led their troops down the Boser Couter in a final charge which swept aside the French

Household Cavalry and Dragoons who tried to rally the routed right wing.

9 p.m.   Darkness saved the French from complete disaster. Overkirk had enveloped the French right; Eugène was round their left flank.   British cavalry on the Allies' right rear were ready to attack the troops on the French left rear north of the River Norken.

Vendôme tried to lead these reserves forward in a last effort to check Eugène's victorious advance.   But panic had set in. Some of the French broke through and retreated through Bevere towards France.   Many of them escaped towards Ghent.   Had there been another two hours of daylight, the bulk of the French Army might have been surrounded, but, owing to the darkness and the fear of the Allies' encircling troops firing into each other, a halt had to be called.

July 12th.—Forty squadrons, followed later by thirty-four battalions, were sent at daybreak to pursue the French Army towards Ghent.   A detachment was also sent to destroy the French lines between Ypres and the River Lys.

This was successfully done.   Another detachment was sent to levy contributions round Arras and Lens.   Tilly also took 12,000 men for a raid into Artois and Picardy.   Vendôme brought in the garrisons of the frontier fortresses to reinforce his field army.

July 15th.—Marlborough's army marched to Wervicq. Vendôme retreated behind the Bruges-Ghent Canal, in order to command the waterways of West Flanders.   Marlborough saw that Vendôme had left open to him the way to the French capital, and that the frontier fortresses would be no barrier to a field army if he could requisition sufficient supplies for his army.

This was quite possible in the fertile district of Artois.   He therefore planned to co-operate with a force which was being got ready to land on the French coast.   At this landing-place, Marlborough would, he hoped, be able to create a fresh base. This scheme was opposed by the Dutch Deputies and by Eugène.   They considered that Lille, the capital of French Flanders, should first be captured.   This strongly fortified place was an important road centre and magazine on the banks of the River Deule.   Marlborough accordingly started to collect the necessary guns and mortars to carry out the siege.

July 23rd.—Eugène's force of forty-three guns and eighteen battalions was at Brussels.

July 28th.—Boufflers entered Lille in order to conduct the siege operations.

August 6th.—Eugène's force started to convoy the hundred guns and mortars via Soignies. Marlborough detached Lottum, with forty squadrons and twenty-four battalions, to meet the convoy. Vendôme sent a detachment towards Alost.

August 8th.—The convoy reached Ath. Neither Vendôme's army nor the troops under Berwick moved to interrupt its march. These two commanders could not agree to a joint plan of action. Vendôme did not wish to attack Brussels or to combine with Berwick in striking at the convoy and in preventing it from reaching Lille. These two forces were admirably situated for any co-operation either against Brussels or against Lille. Vendôme was at Ghent; Berwick was at Mons. These two places are nearly equi-distant from Brussels and Lille. Therefore, it was possible for the two French commanders to combine either to attack Brussels or to intercept the convoy between Brussels and Lille. In either case, they could combine and they could bring superior numbers to bear at the decisive point. This point might have been at Brussels, against the troops besieging Lille, or against the convoy advancing from Brussels to Lille.

August 10th.—The convoy was on the River Scheldt, where it was met by thirty squadrons sent out to meet it by Marlborough.

August 11th.—Marlborough also sent forty-four squadrons and thirty battalions, under the Prince of Orange, from Menin to invest Lille.

Boufflers burnt down all buildings near the outer fortifications of the town, in order to improve the observation and field of fire.

August 12th.—Marlborough, with thirty-seven squadrons and eighty-three battalions, remained at Helchin, on the River Scheldt, in order to cover the siege of Lille.

The convoy reached Marlborough's army at Helchin. Vendôme and Berwick decided to unite their armies at Lessines.

August 19th.—The junction of the French armies between Lessines and Grammont was effected.

August 21st.—The whole French Army advanced to Tournai.

August 22nd.—The French Army crossed the River Scheldt and reached Blandain. The besiegers of Lille strengthened their field defences.

August 24th.—The besiegers made a night attack, and captured an outwork—Marquette Abbey—which was a fortified chapel.

August 26th.—The French recovered the Marquette Abbey, but the besiegers were able to advance and secure the passage of the River Deule north-west of Lille, which was now completely invested.

August 27th.—The Allies began to bombard Lille with their siege artillery of 180 pieces. The French Army moved towards Tournai.

August 30th.—Marlborough marched to Templeuve.

September 1st.—Marlborough marched behind the Marque and took up a position—which was later entrenched—to block the French advance both from Tournai and from Douai.

The two French commanders were undecided as to their further operations. Berwick wished to make a direct attack via Pont-à-Tressin. Vendôme wished to move round by the Douai-Lille Road.

September 5th.—The French advanced, but would not attack the Allies' position.

September 7th.—Our assault on the counterscarp was only partially successful.

September 11th.—The French again advanced. They crossed the Marque and moved to the Lens-Lille Road. After reconnoitring the Allies' position, they withdrew across the River Scheldt.

September 12th.—The Dutch Deputies would not sanction Marlborough's plan to counter-attack.

September 16th.—The French withdrew across the River Scheldt.

September 20th.—The Allies made another attack on Lille, reinforced by 5,000 British troops. This was repulsed with loss. Vendôme now took up a position across the besiegers' communications with Brussels. Marlborough therefore decided to open up Ostend as a sea-borne supply depot.

Erle's detachment, which was to have been sent to Portugal, was diverted to this place. Erle occupied Oudenarde and Leffinghen.

September 27th.—Seven hundred wagons with supplies, escorted by twelve battalions and 1,500 sabres, started from Ostend to join Marlborough's army.

E

Marlborough sent twelve battalions, under Webb, to Thourout, and eighteen squadrons, under Cadogan, to Roulers.

September 28th.—Vendôme sent sixty squadrons and thirty-four battalions, under de la Motte, to Wynendale, to intercept this convoy. Here General Webb took up a position on a narrow front, with both flanks resting on woods in which two battalions were hidden.

When the French attacked, they could not make full use of their superiority of numbers, as their frontage of attack was limited by the woods on either side of Webb's position. The Allies maintained their position during the preliminary artillery fire by the French. When the French advanced, in four dense lines, to the attack, the Allied troops holding the defile of Wynendale opened fire simultaneously from the front and from the flank troops in the two woods. The French were surprised and routed. They retreated with a loss of nearly four thousand casualties and all their artillery. The convoy during and after the action proceeded safely to its destination.

September 29th.—Renewed attacks were made against Lille by the Allies, and the outworks were captured.

October 1st.—The counterscarp of the fortress of Lille was captured.

October 3rd.—Marlborough supervised another attack on Lille. A bastion was captured, so that it became possible to drain off the water in the moat round the main wall.

In order to prevent a second convoy from reaching the Allied Army from Ostend, the French commander decided to cut the communications with this place by cutting the dykes between Bruges and Nieuport, and flooding the country round Ostend and Oudenburg.

Supplies then had to be taken in flat-bottomed boats to Leffinghen, and then taken out of the flooded area in high-wheeled carts. In this way, a convoy of 900 wagons, with 1,700 barrels of gunpowder, safely reached the besieging army. The troops were now put on reduced rations; two days' supplies had to last for three days.

October 21st.—Eugène made a final attack on Lille, supported by the fire of ninety-one pieces.

October 22nd.—Boufflers agreed to surrender the town of Lille. The sick and wounded, also the wives and families of officers and soldiers, and all the cavalry received a free passage to Douai.

Prisoners were exchanged.   The French garrison had to retire into the citadel.

October 25th.—Boufflers retired into the citadel of Lille. Eugène made arrangements to reduce the citadel by sapping.

October 26th.—Marlborough made preparations to force the passage of the River Scheldt.   He divided his army into three columns, in order to cross the river at Escanaffles, Gavre, and Berchem.

October 27th.—Marlborough crossed the River Scheldt as planned, and advanced on Oudenarde, which the French evacuated, leaving their baggage behind.   A thousand French prisoners were captured here.   At Gavre, the French abandoned their guns.   The French, completely surprised by this movement, retired on Ghent, Mons, and Tournai.

October 28th.—Eugène, with his army, returned to Lille. Marlborough, advancing on Brussels, reached Alost.

October 29th.—Marlborough reached Brussels.   The Elector of Bavaria, who had threatened this town, withdrew, leaving behind his wounded and his guns.

December 9th.—The citadel of Lille capitulated.   Eugène's army was now free to co-operate with Marlborough.   They decided to capture Bruges and Ghent, in order to bring the war to an end.

December 1st.—Marlborough's army moved to Bierleghem and Oudenarde.

December 6th.—Marlborough and Eugène were at Melle and Meirelbeke.

December 18th.—Ghent was completely invested by the Allies.   This town was held by thirty-four battalions and twenty squadrons, under de la Motte.

December 29th.—de la Motte capitulated.   Three days later Bruges, Plasschendaele and Leffinghen were evacuated by the French.

CHAPTER IX.

1709.—General Summary of Events.

MARLBOROUGH hoped to secure a favourable peace. Louis XIV was disappointed and discouraged by the results of the 1708 campaign; the French resources were nearly exhausted, and the people were suffering from famine caused by severe wintry weather. However, the demands of the Allies were too onerous to be accepted.

Louis XIV's appeal to the nation to save the country from invasion led to a liberal response, both with men and money, to carry on the war. Their Army was reinforced from other theatres of operation, and was concentrated in Flanders to cover the north-eastern approaches to France via Arras.

This army was placed under the command of Villars, who entrenched himself on the Plain of Lens between the River Scarpe at Douai and the River Lys.

Marlborough remained in England from January to April. When he returned to the Hague, he joined Eugène, and camped south-east of Lille, between Linselles and Fontenoy, with an army consisting of 110,000 men, with which they invested Tournai. The heavy artillery was brought up the River Scheldt from Ghent to this city.

Villars had weakened the garrison, and could do little beyond making demonstrations, as his main army was twenty-five miles away behind his fortified lines. The citadel capitulated on September 3rd. Before this date, however, the Allies had prepared for the investment of Mons.

By means of a forced march of fifty miles in fifty-six hours, they reached a position three miles north-east of Mons. Here the Allied Army was faced by entrenchments, weakly held, between Mons and the River Sambre. In the entrenchments there were gaps in the vicinity of Jemappes and of Malplaquet.

As soon as the Allies advanced, Vendôme sent a detachment to Jemappes, which was the gap nearest to his army's position. He was too late to close it. Marlborough had sent forward troops under the Prince of Hesse-Cassel. They arrived and took up a position before the French reached the vicinity of the gap.

The French detachment then waited for the arrival of their main army, which was not in time to prevent the Allies from investing Mons. Marlborough then left an investing force round Mons, and brought the bulk of his army to Ciply and Quévy.

Villars then took up a position, which was entrenched between the Laignières and Taisnières Woods.

On September 11th, the Allies made an attack on the French position. Eugène, on the right, attacked Villars, and Marlborough, commanding the troops in the centre and left, dealt with Boufflers.

The attack was started by two columns of Marlborough's forces, a feint attack under the Prince of Orange on the left, and another under Schulemberg and Lottum on the right centre and right, where there was heavy fighting round and in Sart and the Tiry Woods.

On the left, Orange turned his feint into an assault, which was successful at first. The forward French fortifications were captured, but, owing to two Dutch Generals and the commander of the Scottish Brigade being killed, and owing to a counter-attack by Boufflers, the Prince of Orange was forced to withdraw. Marlborough restored this situation, and Boufflers did not press his counter-attack.

On the right flank, Eugène was able to maintain the position. In the centre, the situation was restored by Marlborough, who personally led a charge of 3,000 sabres against the French, and saved the situation in front of Count Lottum. After this stage in the battle, Villars took the Irish and Breton brigades from his centre and made an attack against the English troops holding the Taisnières Wood.

Marlborough then attacked the weakened French centre, and gained ground in rear of the French works. This breaking of the French centre enabled the Allies, now reinforced by the troops that had been left behind at Tournai, to drive back the French right, in spite of Villars leading a counter-attack and in spite of Boufflers' attempts to retrieve the disaster to the centre and right of the line.

The French withdrew towards Bavai and Quiévrain. Their losses were 12,000; the Allies lost 20,000.

Mons fell on October 11th. This closed the year's campaign.

1709.—PARTICULAR DATES.

April 9th.—Marlborough reached the Hague, and was joined by Eugène. They decided to besiege Tournai.

June 7th.—The army under Marlborough and Eugène, 110,000 strong, assembled south-east of Lille. Villars, commanding the French troops, took up a strong natural position between Douai on the River Scarpe to St. Venant on the River Lys. The two courses open to Marlborough were to move round Villars's western flank and attack St. Omer or Aire, or to operate against Tournai in the Scheldt Valley.

Villars anticipated that Marlborough would attack him on his left flank and would advance up the River Lys. Marlborough strengthened this idea, by bringing up his siege artillery to Menin.

Villars then weakened Tournai, and brought in available troops to his left flank. Marlborough then decided to make a rapid advance on Tournai.

June 26th.—The Allies left their camp and marched at first towards La Bassée, as if to attack the centre of Villars's position, and then, after dark, direction was changed to the east. The troops marched all night towards Tournai.

June 27th.—Soon after dawn, the Allies reached the walls of Tournai. Its garrison was completely surprised, and Villars had been completely deceived as to the direction of Marlborough's intended operations. He had reduced the garrison of Tournai to 7,000 men, and the arrangements for their provisioning were inadequate.

The investment was commenced. Eugène took up a position to cover the siege between Pont-à-Tressin and St. Amand.

June 29th.—Marlborough's siege artillery arrived at Tournai. Villars strengthened the fortifications on his right flank and at Condé and Valenciennes. The French inundated the country between Tournai, Condé and Mons.

July 26th.—The Allies made an assault on Tournai, and captured many outworks. Villars's troops were in no condition to relieve the situation. They were ill-fed and underpaid. They remained behind his fortifications, but were not able to counter-attack Marlborough's army.

July 30th.—The Governor of Tournai surrendered the town and retired with the bulk of the garrison into the citadel. The Allies now began to sap towards and under the walls of the citadel.

August 8th.—Eugène's covering army moved to a position between Pont-à-Marque and Rumegies, in order to ease the supply situation.

Villars added to his fortifications by extending them in an easterly direction towards the Scarpe at Valenciennes.

September 3rd.—Tournai citadel surrendered. The besiegers had incurred over 5,000 casualties during this siege.

The alternative plans which Marlborough considered were either to force a passage to the Channel ports or to advance by Mons.

The first alternative would necessitate the reduction of Ypres to open his communications with the north; the second alternative, namely, to advance round Villars's eastern flank, was not so attractive strategically, as he could not co-operate with our Navy, but, on the other hand, Mons was weakly held. It was, therefore, decided to march to Mons and to invest it.

Marlborough accordingly on this afternoon (September 3rd) dispatched a detachment, under Orkney, to capture St. Ghislain, five miles west of Mons, and to secure the passage of the River Haine there.   This detachment was followed by another of sixty squadrons and 4,000 infantry, under the Prince of Hesse-Cassel.

The remainder of the army—less a force of twenty-four battalions left to make the arrangements for the final evacuation of Tournai—began to march towards Mons during the night.

September 6th.—At 2 p.m., Hesse-Cassel's detachment began to cross the River Haine at Nimy and Obourg.   Their march was then directed south-west towards the fortified lines which Villars had erected from the south of Mons in a south-easterly direction towards the River Sambre.

Hesse-Cassel was in time to occupy a position between Jemappes and Frameries before the cavalry sent forward by Villars arrived to strengthen the weak garrison which had been forced to withdraw by the Allies' superior numbers, and owing to their unexpected attack.

The Allied Army, followed by Hesse-Cassel's detachment, by the evening had crossed the River Haine and reached a position on the eastern side of Mons.

September 7th.—Villars, with the French Army, arrived in its entrenched positions in the vicinity of Mons, covering the Trouée de Boussu south-west of Jemappes.   Owing to the wooded nature of the country, it was only by these trouées—which are clearings in the woods—that the French Army could advance from its present position towards Mons.

The position of the French Army during the night September 7th/8th was between Athis (eight miles south-west of Jemappes) and Montroeul (eight miles west of Jemappes).

September 8th.—Marlborough's own troops were encamped at Quévy-le-Grand, covering the Trouée d'Aulnois. Eugène's army covered the Trouée de Boussu from the vicinity of Quaregnon.

September 9th.—Villars's army, 95,000 strong, marched towards the Trouée d'Aulnois. This move was discovered and opposed by Marlborough's cavalry under d'Auvergne. Villars, however, was able to drive back the Allied cavalry and to occupy a position on rising ground on a front of 3,000 yards between the Forest of Laignières and the Forest of Taisnières.

With his available forces, Villars might have taken the offensive with superior numbers at the decisive point. But the frontage on which he could advance freely was limited and, therefore, to form up on the far side of the trouée would take considerable time, and it would have been possible for the Allies to have brought up troops to attack the French as they formed into their lines in the open.

On the other hand, Marlborough has been criticized for his delay in attacking Villars before the French had strengthened their position. Every hour the French added to the strength of their works would make the attackers' task more costly and difficult. But the reason was that Marlborough had not yet got up his full strength.

Twenty battalions were still at Tournai, nor was all his artillery with his field army. Eugène's army was not yet in line with Marlborough by the afternoon.

The French position was strong naturally, and to make a frontal attack against superior numbers on the narrow frontage of the Trouée d'Aulnois unsupported by artillery would have been costly and hazardous, especially as there was little time for reconnaissance, and, though it could be seen that the French trenches extended right across the gap between the Laignières and Taisnières Woods, yet Marlborough was uncertain what these woods contained, and how the reserves were posted in the slopes west of their main position.

September 10th.—The investment of Mons was completed. St. Ghislain was attacked in order to gain a direct route for reinforcements from Tournai.

The French positions were reconnoitred during the day. Marlborough had to make his decision as to whether he would attack or not, in view of the strength of the French lines.

His reason for attacking was that he seldom had an opportunity of a pitched battle with the French, and the moral effect of a victory in the field was far greater than the capture of a fortress.

It would have been more prudent to have been content to invest Mons and to wait for Villars to attempt to relieve it by attacking his position north of the trouée, especially as he had not that superiority in men and artillery which would justify the assumption of the offensive with any certainty of success.

Marlborough had a superiority of approximately 20,000 infantry and 20 guns, whereas the French had ten more squadrons of cavalry and the advantage of a very strong position.

If Marlborough decided to continue only with the siege of Mons, Villars would then have been in the difficult position of having to decide to attack or to remain inactive, with the Allies in his front storming another of his towns, which must then fall unless it was relieved.

Marlborough, however, decided to take a risk and attack, in order to gain the advantage of a victory in the field.   He knew that he could rely on the loyal co-operation of Eugène and of his troops, and he was confident that he could gain a victory.

Villars had his right wing under Boufflers.   This wing was posted in the Bois de Laignières and the trenches in the trouée west of it.   In this wing were forty-five battalions in the most easterly positions, then a further seventeen battalions with twenty guns continued the line to the centre of the trouée.

The left wing was under Villars.   It stretched in the left centre to the edge of the Forest of Sart.   In this area there were seventeen battalions.   Then twenty-three battalions continued the line along the edges of the Forest of Sart, with seventeen more in reserve behind the wood; the sixty remaining guns were posted at intervals along the left centre and in the forests.

September 11th.—The plan of attack was that the left flank of the French position was to be first attacked and then a frontal assault was to be made against the entrenchments in the trouée.   The attack from the north against the French left flank in the salient of the Forest of Sart was to be made by fifty-eight battalions, whose left would be protected by fifteen British battalions.

The Prince of Orange had thirty battalions under his command for action against the French troops in the Forest of Laignières.

The bulk of Marlborough's hundred guns were distributed in two positions—one of twenty-eight guns to support his left attack, one of forty guns to support his right attack. The remainder of the artillery was distributed along his front. The cavalry were in rear of the infantry.

On this day, the 18th Royal Irish, at the head of Withers's force, arrived at the psychological moment to help to defeat the counter-attack of Villars's eighty battalions west of the clearing of the Trouée d'Aulnois. Among Villars's troops was the Irish Brigade, which had been fighting for Louis XIV.

9 a.m. The attacking columns and the guns were in position. The guns opened fire on the French left wing, and the battalions, formed in three lines, started to advance to the attack in accordance with the plan.

The attack against the French right wing was to be a demonstration. A thick mist had helped to hide the movements of the Allies, and in the centre of the trouée they also gained cover and concealment from the Tiry Wood. The attack against the French northern flank was brought to a standstill by the troops in this area, who maintained their position.

Reinforcements were brought up, but the swampy nature of the ground in front of the French entrenchments in the Sart Wood made progress slow and difficult, and prevented any possibility of surprise.

Owing to the lack of success by our force, under Schulemberg and under Lottum, Orkney's troops on the right centre of the position protecting Lottum's left flank came under heavy fire from the edge of the Sart Forest.

Orkney's original orders had been to move forward on Lottum's left, but not to make an attack until the forest on his right had been cleared. However, he disobeyed these instructions by sending two battalions into the wood to counter-attack the troops on Lottum's flank.

Marlborough supported this reinforced attack with thirty squadrons, which he led personally. As the infantry advanced a second time to attack the enemy in the salient of Sart Forest, twelve French battalions left their entrenchments and charged forward to make a counter-attack.

Villars, fearing that Marlborough would lead the cavalry to a counter-attack, ordered them to return to their trenches. Then the Allied infantry were able to make progress and to attack on more equal terms.

Gradually the pressure of combined attacks of Schulemberg's thirty-six battalions on the northern face of the salient held by the French in the Sart Forest, and the twenty-two battalions under Lottum against its eastern face, made itself felt, and the

French were gradually driven back, after very stubborn hand-to-hand fighting, through the wood to the open ground beyond.

Boufflers, on the right flank, was unable to spare reinforcements, as he was being fiercely attacked in the Forest of Laignières by the Prince of Orange.

This commander, who had been ordered to make a feint attack against the French right, exceeded his instructions and led forward all his thirty battalions to capture the French trenches by a frontal attack.   He was successful at first in gaining their first line, but their second line did not give way, and the Dutch troops became disordered.

When the Navarre troops counter-attacked, the Allies were driven back on to Hesse-Cassel's supporting cavalry.

Boufflers luckily did not follow up this successful counter-attack, in spite of his superiority of numbers in this area of the battlefield.   He was unaware of the exact dispositions and numbers opposed to him, owing to the Tiry Wood in his front behind which the Allies might be able to conceal reinforcements.   Their movements could not be seen, and he anticipated that there would be more troops in the vicinity owing to the vigour and determination of the repeated attacks made by the Prince of Orange.

Had Boufflers counter-attacked with all available forces under his command, he could have turned the retreat of Orange's troops into a rout.

Marlborough, on reaching this part of the field with a few battalions hastily collected, was able to restore the situation. He ordered the Prince of Orange to maintain his position, but not to attack again until pressure had been brought to bear against Boufflers' right flank.

On returning to his northern flank, Marlborough found that Villars had been able to avert disaster and to check the Allies' advance by weakening his centre and reinforcing his left flank with the troops drawn from the trenches in the trouée.   In this way, Villars was able to collect some fifty battalions, which he meant to lead himself in a counter-attack.

But luckily, just at this time, General Withers's troops, with the 18th Royal Irish Regiment at their head, arrived on the Allies' right flank with the twenty battalions from Tournai. It was at this moment that Villars's counter-attack with eighty battalions, in which were the Irish Brigade, was taking effect and was driving back Schulemberg and Lottum that Withers struck his left flank, and, at practically the same time, Villars was wounded in the knee.   He had to be taken from the field.

His absence and the consequent lack of direction of operations were greatly felt.

Eugène now led the advance against the French left flank, and slowly, after much hand-to-hand fighting, the French were forced to withdraw.

Eugène was wounded in the head, but he continued to lead the troops.   The French opposed to him were only saved by drawing troops from their centre to arrest his advance in conjunction with Withers's flank attack.

1 p.m.   This was now the opportunity for Marlborough to strike with all available troops at the decisive place, namely, the weakened French centre.   He ordered Orkney to attack the French trenches in the trouée north-east of Malplaquet. This operation he supported with the fire of forty guns.

At the first assault, Orkney's troops carried the forward trenches.   He then formed up his lines again and renewed his attacks, and carried all the remaining French trenches in the centre of their position.   The Dutch cavalry closely supporting the infantry followed up and passed the trenches into the open west of Malplaquet.

Here in turn they were counter-attacked by the French Gendarmerie under Boufflers, and were driven back into Orkney's infantry, who were now manning the trenches which they had captured in their second assault.   The Gendarmerie were checked, and, as Orange's men came up into line with Orkney's troops, were forced to withdraw.

This withdrawal was hastened by the charge of Prussian and British cavalry.

Boufflers then used up his last reserve with a charge of the French Household Cavalry.   Their attack was at first successful, but Eugène then led his cavalry into the fight and drove back the French horse.

The Prince of Hesse at the same time co-operated by sending in all his available cavalry and infantry against the French right flank, and succeeded in driving the troops on this flank away from their troops fighting in the centre.

Boufflers, after leading six unsuccessful attacks in the centre of his position, gave orders for his whole army to retire on Quiévrain and Bavai.

The French retreat was not followed up by the Allies, who were too much exhausted to pursue, and the reserves who might have been available for pursuit had been used up by Orange's attack against the French right wing.   His disobedience of Marlborough's order in making a premature attack not only led to heavy casualties, but used up his own troops and reserves required to restore the situation.

Had these reserves been available when Boufflers' final charges had been driven back, the full results of the victory might have been gained by a vigorous and sustained pursuit.

Their casualties had been nearly twice as many as those of the French, who had lost 12,000 men.   This victory had been most costly for the Allies, but it again proved the military superiority of their commanders and troops over their enemies, and it caused the French to be driven out of Brabant and Flanders.

September 14th.—The Allies began to besiege Mons actively. The French made no efforts to relieve this place.

October 9th.—Siege artillery was brought up by the Allies from Brussels.

October 11th.—Mons fell.   Owing to wet weather, and, consequently, to the state of the roads and of the country, and owing to the difficulty of obtaining forage, the Allied troops now went into winter quarters.

BATTLES DESCRIBED IN CONJUNCTION WITH THE FIELD SERVICE
REGULATIONS, VOL. II.
BLENHEIM.—August 13th, 1704.
RAMILLIES.—May 23rd, 1706.
OUDENARDE.—July 11th, 1708.
MALPLAQUET.—September 11th, 1709.

CHAPTER X

BATTLE OF BLENHEIM, AUGUST 13TH, 1704.

" Detailed and timely information about the enemy and
the theatre of operations is a necessary factor of success
in war." [F.S.R. 33 (1).]

Marlborough and Eugène realized the importance of information, and accordingly they made a personal reconnaissance on
August 12th. They went forward to Tapfheim, west of the
Kessel River. From a church tower at this place they could
see the preparations of the Franco-Bavarian Army for a camp
west of the River Nebel. They were able to make their
appreciation of the situation and their deductions on the ground
and it was in time to be of use. In F.S.R. 33 (9) it is stated
that " the value of information depends on whether it is
relevant and reaches the authorities concerned in time to be
of use."

The Allied commanders fully realized that, if their enemies
were intending to camp west of the River Nebel, there would
be little time for them to fortify their position by the time
they could be attacked on the following day. Therefore, if
prompt measures were taken for offensive action on the 13th,
it might be possible to surprise the French before they had
entrenched their position. In F.S.R. 37, it is also stated:

" Every commander should obtain by personal reconnaissance as thorough a grasp as time will allow of the
ground over which his troops may become engaged and
the topographical difficulties which they may encounter.
Time spent in reconnaissance is seldom wasted."

Marlborough's time was most profitably spent in observing the enemy's position and the ground which his army would have to cross in order to reach it.   He noted that, if he made a frontal attack north of Blenheim, the River Nebel, with its marshy sides, would be a considerable obstacle.

Also that, if the French occupied a five-mile front from Blenheim to Lutzingen—and this appeared to be indicated from their preliminary arrangements—it would be impossible to out-flank their position on the south, owing to the River Danube, and the woods on the north of Lutzingen would make a con-siderable detour necessary if an enveloping movement was to be attempted on this flank.   Marlborough was able to appre-ciate the risks of attacking this strong position held by approximately 53,000 men with his army of 160 squadrons and sixty-six battalions.   There was the additional disadvantage that he had thirty less guns than the Franco-Bavarian Army.

Marlborough could appreciate the difficulty of attacking such a strong position with his available forces, but he realized that, if he delayed, Tallard, the opposing commander, would strengthen his position, and every hour might add to the diffi-culties of an assault, nor could the Allies become any stronger until the fall of Ingolstadt released Prince Louis of Baden and his army.   Also he had made this march, to the Danube from the Rhine, with the purpose of bringing his enemy to battle in the field.

He had gained a great strategic advantage by reaching his present position.   Tallard was unaware of his strength and intentions.   He would, therefore, be able to gain a tactical surprise by striking as early as possible, and, unless the Franco-Bavarian Army was defeated now before there was time to entrench, he would have difficulty in maintaining his position, owing to the supply situation, which might be made more difficult if Villeroy began to operate in Wurtemburg and to interrupt his communications with the Rhine.   Such a course of action by his enemy would make it impossible for him to remain on the Danube during the winter.

He had information on which to base his plan of attack as laid down in F.S.R. 38.   He could estimate the extent of Tallard's position, the weak parts, the defended localities, the obstacles, the best line of attack, and the best forming-up position for attacking troops.

There could be no more favourable opportunity for attack, and Marlborough, fully realizing the risks, had full confidence in his tactical skill, and he therefore decided to carry out his plan on the 13th, so that his successful strategy could be crowned with tactical victory.

While Tallard was preparing to strengthen his line and to put Blenheim, Oberglauheim and Lutzingen in a state of defence, Marlborough decided to take the initiative while Tallard was still in the open and within his reach, and to make his attack early on August 13th.   This was in accordance with F.S.R. 8:

" The commander holding the initiative will make every effort to prevent the operations becoming stabilized."

Marlborough acted on the principle that
" The ultimate aim, which is the destruction of the enemy's main forces, must always be held in view, and all other undertakings subordinated to this."   [F.S.R. 5 (3).]

He also appreciated the necessity of considering questions of policy, relative strengths and relative readiness for action as advocated in Field Service Regulations.

He himself supplied the necessary courage, energy and determination and the bold offensive spirit which F.S.R. (2) indicate as essential for success in war.   In his army was the necessary " organization, discipline and training which his skilful and resolute leading would turn to the fullest account."

Having balanced, in consultation with Eugène, the advantages and disadvantages of the situation, Marlborough was prepared to accept responsibility and to make his decision.

" The chief rôle of a commander is to make decisions." [F.S.R. 10 (4).]

The following paragraph, F.S.R. 10 (2), might have been specially written about Marlborough:

" The essential characteristics of a commander are a strong and resolute will and a ready acceptance of responsibility.   He must have ability, clear judgment and a well-balanced sense of proportion.   He must also have a temperament which is neither unduly elated by success nor depressed by failure.   These characteristics should be supported by a thorough knowledge and deep study of war.   It is the consciousness of knowledge which ensures self-confidence and enables a commander to judge situations on their merits rather than in accordance with any fixed formulæ."

Marlborough's resolution, ready acceptance of responsibility, clear judgment and self-confidence were conspicuous in this battle.

Tallard, on the other hand, had no clear idea as to how

victories can be won. The destruction of his enemy's main forces to obtain decisive results did not enter into his calculations. He did not realize that " victory can be won only as a result of offensive action." [F.S.R. 88 (1).] Nor did he realize that in defence " the first requirement will be information." [F.S.R. 90 (1).]

Neither Tallard nor his subordinates Marsin and the Elector of Bavaria made personal reconnaissances. Nor were cavalry or other troops sent ahead to gain information.

Even as late as the morning of August 13th, when the Allies had gained contact with his outposts, Tallard thought that they were retiring. Tallard then took up a naturally strong position, but it was not in accordance with our accepted teaching, as laid down in our F.S.R., which state that

" The defensive, if an offensive spirit inspires its conduct, may effectively create a favourable opportunity for resuming the offensive, and may prepare the way for defeating the enemy when the general situation is more favourable."

In this case, in the Franco-Bavarian Army there was no offensive spirit; there was no provision for a counter-stroke either with reserves of men or in the position, along the front of which ran the River Nebel, which added to the strength of the position for its passive occupation, but not for the assumption of the offensive.

The following passage from F.S.R. 89 (1) was not in accordance with Tallard's views on defence :

" The ground in front of the position should be suitable for the assumption of the offensive, and unless the counter-stroke is to be carried out by reinforcements which have not yet arrived the extent of the position taken up should not be so great as to reduce the number of men kept in hand for offensive action much below half the total force at his disposal. The most favourable ground for the ultimate assumption of the offensive is that which lends itself to the co-operation of all arms."

The position which Tallard had occupied was as close as possible to the obstacle of the River Nebel, which afforded a considerable protection against any enemy advancing from the east. However, we are warned in F.S.R. 90 (2) that :

" The strength of a defensive position will depend not so much upon the natural advantages of the ground as upon the *morale* of the defending troops and the degree

F

to which their resistance can be organized in accordance with a well co-ordinated scheme embodying the close co-operation of all arms.''

Tallard overcrowded the village of Blenheim with twenty-seven battalions when he had entrenched it as strongly as possible, and he placed twelve dismounted squadrons south of the villages. He thus sacrificed their mobility to passive defence, and he relied on the strength of his position and to his numbers to hold his right flank. In Oberglauheim village, which was strengthened, he placed eight battalions; at Lutzingen, which was also fortified, five battalions were posted.

By thus immobilizing the bulk of his force to hold entrenched localities, Tallard was not making his defence resilient, and he was relying more on the natural strength of his position than on the *morale* and fighting efficiency of his troops. In occupying his position, Tallard did not carry out the principles embodied in F.S.R. 88 (3):

> '' The object of the defending troops is to inflict the maximum loss on the enemy at the least expense to themselves and so to wear down his fighting power, while maintaining their own, that they will be able at a suitable time to resume the offensive and complete his defeat.''

Tallard did not have his troops in the centre of his position so disposed on the banks of the River Nebel that they could dispute the actual passage of the river. His position would have been more secure had he done this, as the Allies must have suffered heavily if he had covered the crossing-places with his close and effective fire. They could have done this at the least expense to themselves, as the Allies could only have crossed the river and the marshes on either side of it very slowly, while the French would have been able to keep them under a continuous fire.

Mounted troops farther west could have been available to charge down hill and take advantage of the Allies' disorganization after crossing, and of their difficulty in forming up for a further advance after crossing this obstacle.

In addition, troops crossing to the west of the River Nebel in the centre of Tallard's position would have on their flanks the strongly held posts at Blenheim and Oberglauheim. Therefore, Tallard had a more than ordinarily strong, natural position, of which he did not take full advantage to inflict the maximum loss on his enemy.

The disposition of Tallard's forces in lines throughout a front of nearly five miles did not enable him to have a well co-ordinated scheme in which his arms could co-operate, and was not in accordance with F.S.R. 90 (2). Nor was there the depth to his position to enable him to make a resilient defence.

There was a good view in front of the position over the ground by which the enemy must advance. The position selected on the line Blenheim-Lutzingen was strategically important, as it blocked the Allies' march up the Danube. There was excellent ground in rear of the position in the plain north of Hochstadt, in which the local and other reserves could move unseen from the east of the ridge on which the Franco-Bavarian Army was formed up between Blenheim and Lutzingen.

These points fulfil the requirements for a defensive position, as laid down in F.S.R. 88 (3) and 89 (7). But in F.S.R. 88 (3) it is also stated that :

> " Everything possible must be done to economize man-power in the defence, in order that the maximum power may be available for eventual offensive action.

> " In arranging for the disposition of a given force, a balance must be struck between the frontage taken up and the depth to which the force is distributed."

In this case, Tallard had not considered sufficiently the disposition of his force in depth, nor the distribution of his troops to give him the maximum power for offensive action.

As has been already stated, he crowded troops into Blenheim and Oberglauheim, so that for his centre he had only nine battalions and five more with which to extend his left flank to Lutzingen. He formed up eighty squadrons in two lines on a two-mile front along the ridge between Blenheim and Oberglauheim, and more cavalry, in two lines, was used up to cover the position to Lutzingen. This method of cavalry holding the crest of the glacis slope of the ridge west of the Nebel River along the main position was quite contrary to our present ideas in making full use always of the mobility of cavalry in every phase of the operations. They were not concealed and concentrated, so that they could make use of the valuable factor of surprise, or so that they could exploit success or be used for any emergency. They were definitely committed to the defence of a part of the line, and thus full use could not be made of their mobility.

The following paragraph in F.S.R. 95 shows the difference between our ideas as to the handling of cavalry to-day and in the time of Marlborough's campaign :

F2

" Until the opposing forces are in close contact the cavalry, supported by other mobile troops when necessary, will be usefully employed in protecting the defensive position.   They must endeavour to mislead the hostile commander as to the exact situation and strength of the position, induce him to deploy prematurely and to fatigue his troops in groping for skilfully concealed flanks, and delay him so as to permit the defensive arrangements to be perfected.   As the opposing force draws near, the mounted troops will be withdrawn.   They should then be assembled in positions selected by the superior commander, where they have scope for action in accordance with his plans."

Tallard had his artillery distributed along his front.   To-day, artillery in defence is distributed in depth, and is allotted to sectors in accordance with the importance of the positions to be defended.   [F.S.R. 94 (1).]

On the side of the Allies, not even the enemies and detractors of Marlborough could find anything but praise to say about his conduct of the operations.   He made his plan, and he maintained his objective throughout the wavering fortunes of the day.

He inspired confidence and maintained the *morale* of his troops by his personal leading.

His actions complied with the following in F.S.R. 11 (1):

" Leadership requires personal courage, high intelligence, sound judgment, an intuitive faculty, and great resolution.   The influence of the leader is chief amongst the moral factors which sway an army."

Throughout the battle, he gave directions for all important situations.   He was always in the place where he was wanted, because he was vigilant, and knew where the difficulties in the conduct of his operations would be.   His coolness in danger, his self-confidence in dealing with difficulties, his presence of mind under fire gained for him the admiration and confidence of his troops, and the co-operation of his subordinate leaders.   He saw the failure of the frontal assaults first by Rowe's brigade and then by Ferguson's brigade on Blenheim; he realized the strength of the enemy, and stopped any further attacks and useless loss of life until pressure was brought to bear on Blenheim by the passage of the Nebel farther north.   His personal intervention with three battalions and a battery, brought up from near Weilheim, in the fighting round Oberglauheim saved the situation when Blainville's Irish contingent counter-attacked and drove back the two leading battalions of the Prince of Holstein-Beck's brigade.

It was Marlborough himself, at 5 p.m., who led the two lines of cavalry at the critical moment in the battle when the progress of his infantry had been arrested in the centre.   His prompt action rallied his infantry and drove back Tallard's squadrons.

It was Marlborough who, seeing the gap then made in his enemies' lines, led the bulk of his cavalry across the plain to Sonderheim in pursuit of the retreating French horse, with the result that the French commander was captured and the right wing of the French Army was routed.

His final decisive stroke was the result of a definite plan persistently carried through in spite of the enemy's temporary successes, in spite of his own reverses in certain parts of the field, and owing to his continued perseverance to the course of action which he knew would lead to victory.

In all the fluctuations of the battle, Marlborough maintained the offensive spirit of his troops in accordance with F.S.R. 11 (4):

> " The longer and more obstinate the fight, the more marked will become the depression and inertia of the men.
>
> " The leader must rise superior to this moral drag, and must inspire the troops with his own determination."

In the conduct of this battle, Marlborough carried out a sound and simple plan with skill and vigour, as advocated in F.S.R. 67 (1).   Also there was good co-operation between the various components of the force ordered to put the plan into effect, as laid down in F.S.R. 69 (10).

The plan was for Cutts's brigades to attack Blenheim, for Holstein-Beck's troops to attack Oberglauheim, for Eugène to engage Marsin and the Elector about Lutzingen, while Marlborough's main body pressed the attack against the centre of the position.   This was in accordance with F.S.R. 67 (1):

> " Each body of troops assigned to a distinct tactical operation must be placed under one commander."

It was essential to ensure that these operations should be simultaneous, so that full pressure throughout could be exerted on the enemy's troops, and so that they could not weaken one part in order to reinforce another.   On this subject it is stated in F.S.R. 67 (1):

" It is essential that arrangements should be made to ensure that attacks intended to be simultaneous are so in reality. This requires close co-operation between the commander concerned and co-ordination by the higher formation."

Tallard had not carried out the principles laid down in F.S.R. 55 (2) for protection at rest, namely:

" A force can be regarded as secure from surprise only when every body of the enemy within striking distance is so closely watched that it can make no movement which does not immediately become known to the outposts. Information will be obtained by the outposts by: (i) Keeping a close watch on all bodies of the enemy within reach of the outposts; (ii) Watching all approaches along which the enemy might advance."

The Allies began their march at 2 a.m. from their bivouac east of the River Kessel, and their nine columns of sixty-six battalions and 160 squadrons reached the high ground east of the River Nebel about Unterglauheim before the French advanced detachments knew that Marlborough's forces were in the vicinity. Tallard's army appears to have been completely surprised, as the signal for the troops to man their posts and for outposts and the foragers to rejoin their units did not sound until after 7 a.m., when battle positions were hurriedly occupied under cover of their guns posted along their whole front.

Marlborough's approach march and then his deployment near Unterglauheim were in accordance with F.S.R. 80 (3):

" The attacking infantry will usually be deployed in close proximity to the enemy's forward defences before the moment fixed for the attack begins. The success or failure of the whole operation may well depend upon the manner in which the approach march and deployment are carried out."

Luckily also for the Allies, Tallard had not carried out the principles in F.S.R. 92 (2, iii). He did not reduce the number of troops required for the security of points tactically essential to the defence by improving their natural tactical value so as to force the enemy into avenues raked by artillery fire. Nor was " the distribution of troops designed to ensure mutual support throughout the system." [F.S.R. 92 (2, iii).]

Tallard did not fully utilize the obstacle of the River Nebel and did not dispute the crossings. This river in the centre of his line with the ridge west of it were the key to the Oberglauheim position. The villages of Blenheim and Oberglauheim were too far apart to enable artillery in their vicinity to reach troops crossing midway between these villages.

The river, with the morasses on either side of it, was a considerable obstacle, and the troops crossing could only move slowly, and would throughout be exposed to the fire of any defenders by the river, and to this they could not reply with covering fire, owing to the width of the obstacle.

Eugène had great difficulty in reaching his appointed forming-up position from which to attack, and there was much delay caused by crossing the many ditches and dykes. Marlborough, however, patiently waited till after midday, when he was in position to ensure the co-operation of united assaults on the enemy's whole front.

Tallard made no attempt to seize the initiative, but he was able to organize the defences of Blenheim, Oberglauheim, and Lutzingen [*vide* F.S.R. 69 (1)].

During this period of waiting for Eugène to get his army into line, the Royal Engineers carried out the duties assigned to them in F.S.R. 84 (3):

" Prior to the attack: (*a*) Skilled work in the forward area to facilitate the approach march and the deployment of the attacking troops; this will include engineer reconnaissance, clearance of obstacles and demolitions; (*b*) main communications and forward tracks, including bridging."

They made five pontoon bridges across the River Nebel to facilitate the Allies' advance between Blenheim and Oberglauheim.

Under Marlborough's personal direction, the artillery support for Eugène's advance was adequate, in accordance with F.S.R. 72 (1):

" Superiority of fire is essential to the successful conduct of the attack and artillery fire affords the most important means to this end. Infantry cannot advance against even semi-organized resistance unless that resistance is kept under subjection by fire power."

Marlborough was " faced with the alternative of either enveloping one or both hostile flanks or making a direct attack with a view to penetration." [F.S.R. 69 (3).] In this case, owing to the strength of the flanks of the position, respectively at Blenheim and Lutzingen, Marlborough decided to make his decisive attack in the greatest possible strength at the enemy's centre.

The battle started with a general advance at 12.45 p.m., the first contact with the enemy being made at Blenheim at 1 p.m. and at Oberglauheim, while Marlborough sent forward his main body across the River Nebel.   This was in four lines; seventeen battalions were forward troops, eleven battalions were in rear with open ranks, with the seventy-one squadrons in two lines between the infantry.

The first brigade sent forward by Cutts to attack Blenheim was repulsed by the greatly superior numbers of the French holding a strongly fortified position.   The French cavalry then charged them as they withdrew in flank.

> " They acted with the greatest dash and resolution to take advantage of fleeting opportunities of intervening in the battle."   [F.S.R. 74.]

Cutts checked the French cavalry with his second line of infantry.   He was on the spot, and so was able to intervene at a critical moment by giving orders, which enabled him to co-operate with Marlborough's main plan.   This was in accordance with F.S.R. 69 (5):

> " The greatest possible strength should be deployed for the decisive attack.   While preparations for this attack are being made and during the attack the enemy should be held to his ground in other parts of the front, and efforts should be made to force him to dissipate his reserves.   Attacks of this nature must be carried out with vigour if they are to fulfil their purpose."

Cutts certainly carried out his attacks vigorously, in order to hold the French to their ground while Marlborough was crossing the River Nebel, in order to penetrate the centre of the enemy's position.

Immediately his first assault failed, he sent forward his other brigade to endeavour to force a way through the enemy's palisades and into Blenheim.   He was able to gain some ground and to press the enemy into the village, but at great loss.

Marlborough now saw that the enemy's superiority in numbers in this quarter enabled them to hold their position against the troops he could spare for this assault.   He therefore ordered Cutts to break off the attack, and so to avoid useless loss of life, but he ordered him to maintain sufficient pressure to prevent the enemy from issuing from Blenheim and reinforcing another part of the field.

This was so effectively done by Cutts and his brigade, that later, when Tallard sent to Blenheim to ask for troops to assist his hard-pressed centre, the commander replied that he could only hold the village.

Marlborough saw that, if the garrison of Blenheim was kept in its position by a brigade, he would immobilize nearly a third of the infantry of Tallard's army, and he could then concentrate superior numbers at the decisive point, and by capturing the ridge between Blenheim and Oberglauheim, and then advancing south-west over the plain towards the Danube, Blenheim must fall and its garrison would be cut off or forced to surrender without the heavy loss of life entailed by frontal attacks.

On his right flank at Oberglauheim, Marlborough had to restore the situation by sending reinforcements of three infantry battalions and some guns, as the attack made by the Prince of Holstein-Beck failed.

The enemy's cavalry charged his infantry, while Marsin's infantry attacked their flank. Though our troops suffered heavily from the attacks of the hostile Irish regiments, yet they managed to maintain a position in front of the village. Farther north, Eugène's attack by 2 p.m. became effective about Lutzingen, and relieved pressure from our troops farther south, as the enemy at first were driven back with a loss of six guns.

The Bavarian cavalry at once carried out the principles laid down in F.S.R. 97 (1), by making an immediate counter-attack to restore the situation and to inflict heavy casualties on the attacking troops. They charged the advancing Imperial Cavalry in flank, and drove them back from the captured guns. The withdrawal of the cavalry exposed the flank of the Danish infantry, who withdrew back to a position east of the River Nebel.

Eugène then rallied his troops and sent forward again the Imperial Cavalry, but the Bavarian cavalry attacked them vigorously, and they lost heavily from the fire of troops on both flanks as they tried to cross the River Nebel.

Eugène now himself led forward the infantry under his command. He was thus carrying out the principle laid down in F.S.R. 11 (4):

> " A leader's greatest difficulty in battle will often lie in maintaining the impetus and offensive power of his troops."

Eugène was able to lead forward his infantry and again to attack the Bavarians in Lutzingen, where he gained ground and was able to prevent any troops from his front being moved to reinforce other parts of the field.

By 4 p.m. no decision had been reached on either side, and, though Tallard had made no effort to seize the initiative, he had maintained his position.

Marlborough by this time, however, had definitely located the weak part of the position. The centre of Tallard's line, being held mainly by cavalry, was now the objective which he meant to capture. Some guns were brought across the River Nebel, in order to give close support in accordance with F.S.R. 72 (1), which states that "the artillery should assist the other arms to maintain their mobility and drive home the attack by every means in its power."

The opposing infantry on both sides were first engaged. The Allied infantry, supported by cavalry and artillery, fought their way up the ridge west of the River Nebel. As soon as the fight was taken to the top of the ridge, Marlborough formed up 8,000 sabres in two lines, the charge was sounded, and they swept on through the opposing infantry and against the French cavalry, who made no use of their mobility, but waited for the charge and then fired with their pistols.

The impetus of the charging troops drove back the French cavalry. Their infantry were thus isolated, and were attacked by superior numbers of the Allied infantry, and also were charged by the cavalry.

When the infantry had been cut down, the cavalry pressed on again after the French cavalry, which Tallard was trying to rally. He could get no help from his troops engaged at Oberglauheim and Blenheim. His demoralized horsemen did not wait for another charge from the Allied cavalry. Most of them retired in disorder across the plain towards Hochstadt and Sonderheim.

In their scramble across the bridge at Hochstadt, a great number were drowned in the Danube, as the bridge collapsed under their weight. The Allied cavalry had acted in accordance with the principle laid down for their action in the attack in F.S.R. 74 (2):

"Cavalry when once committed to decisive action must make the fullest possible use of its mobility and act with the greatest dash and resolution."

The Allied infantry of the centre during this last cavalry charge joined up with Cutts's brigade round Blenheim and attacked this place from the south and the north until it was completely surrounded.

The 9,500 men who formed the garrison of Blenheim, after a short fight, then surrendered. In the north of the battlefield, too, the Franco-Bavarians were isolated and their southern flank was exposed. The Elector and Marsin set fire to Oberglauheim and Lutzingen, and were able to withdraw before they were closely engaged.

The reason for this was that it took a little time to disengage a part of the Allied cavalry from those engaged in the pursuit towards Hochstadt, and Eugène's cavalry were still re-forming east of the River Nebel. This was not in accordance with F.S.R. 74 (1), in which the tasks of cavalry in the attack are summarized and include "Maintenance of pressure on the enemy if he shows signs of withdrawing," and F.S.R. 74 (2): "No consideration can be paid to exhaustion of man or horse until the final overthrow of the enemy is achieved."

The part of the Allied cavalry, withdrawn from the pursuit to the Danube to deal with the retreating French left flank, was unable to distinguish in the dusk Eugène's troops from the Bavarians, and the result was that the Elector and Marsin were able to retire in good order with their guns and baggage towards Morslingen. The Franco-Bavarian Army was assembled here before falling back to Dillingen.

This great victory was won by the commander who "possessed in a greater degree that indomitable resolution and energy which enabled the decision, once made, to be carried through."

Tallard, by failing to gain adequate information on which to base his plan, by allowing the Allies to cross the formidable obstacle of the River Nebel unopposed, by not making use of the mobility of his cavalry, and by relying on the strength of positions and not on the close co-operation of all his arms in the field, and by not attempting to take the initiative, enabled Marlborough to inflict on him a crushing defeat at a cost of less than a third of the casualties incurred by the Franco-Bavarian forces.

Marlborough had not hesitated in maintaining his objective in every crisis throughout the day, and had carried through his final decisive attack with resolution and energy until his enemy was driven from the field.

CHAPTER XI.

Battle of Ramillies, May 23rd, 1706.

In this battle, the following principles of war are strikingly illustrated, namely:

Maintenance of the objective; surprise; concentration; co-operation; and, finally, offensive action by which victory can only be won.

Marlborough, as usual, made his personal reconnaissance, in accordance with F.S.R. 37:

> "Every commander should obtain by personal reconnaissance as thorough a grasp as time will allow of the ground over which his troops may become engaged and the topographical difficulties which they may encounter. Time spent in reconnaissance is rarely wasted."

When Marlborough reconnoitred the position occupied by the French, he realized that his first objective must be the ridge, 2,400 yards long, between Taviers and Ramillies. He was, however, too late to forestall the French on this ridge, as, by 8 a.m., when the advance guard of the Allies reached Merdorp, the French were already in the Plain of Mont St. André, west of Ramillies.

In spite of the advantage of ground which the French had in their favour, in spite of the fact that the numbers on both sides were nearly equal, and in spite of the first attack by Auverquerque, leading the Allied cavalry, being unsuccessful, Marlborough continued with his offensive plan.

The French, by 10 a.m. on May 23rd, had occupied this ridge, with their right flank resting on Taviers and their left flank on Autréglise Their two lines of troops were posted in front of the Tomb of Ottomond and past Ramillies and Offus. Villeroy's position was a strong one, and it had been occupied before the Allies' line of advance had been foreseen. No force was kept in hand for the assumption of the offensive, nor was the conduct of the defence framed to surprise the attackers in accordance with a well co-ordinated scheme embodying the close co-operation of all arms. The result was that, when Marlborough took the initiative by advancing on Francqnée, Villeroy could only counter this movement by sending two battalions and some dragoons to their assistance.

76

Thus he isolated more troops from his main body, and weakened his main force, and early began to conform to Marlborough's operations.

These reinforcing battalions and dragoons were charged by the Allies' supporting cavalry and were routed. Again, on the northern flank, where Marlborough planned to mystify and mislead the Franco-Bavarian forces west of the Little Geete, by sending forward Orkney with twelve battalions to cross the river and to advance on Offus, Villeroy again conformed to Marlborough's operations, and brought troops from his centre to his left, and from his right flank to take the place of those sent to Offus.

This movement was undertaken because Villeroy had not carried out the principles enunciated in F.S.R. 90 (1) and (2) for defence:

> "The first requirement will be information. The force should not be deployed until the enemy's line of advance can be foreseen. A force which is kept in hand covered by the necessary protective troops is able to assume the offensive at once should a favourable opportunity offer itself, or, alternatively, to dispose its troops to the best advantage with a view to accepting battle. The strength of a position will depend not so much upon the natural advantages of the ground as upon the *morale* of the defending troops and the degree to which their resistance can be organized in accordance with a well co-ordinated scheme embodying the close co-operation of all arms."

Villeroy made no attempt to surprise the attackers, and, by conforming to Marlborough's actions, his will became subordinated to the indomitable resolution and energy of his opponent who, having made his decision, carried it through.

The following paragraph in F.S.R. is now applicable:

> "War is a contest between the will of the opposing commanders; given reasonably equal conditions, success will be attained by the commander who possesses a greater degree of that indomitable resolution and energy which enables the decision, once made, to be carried through."

As soon as Villeroy had conformed to Marlborough's feint on his right flank across the Little Geete, Orkney was withdrawn to the eastern side of the river, so that troops could be taken from his command if required at the decisive time and place for the capture of the ridge between Taviers and Ramillies.

Marlborough was able to withdraw one of the lines of infantry from this flank unseen by the enemy behind the ridge east of the Little Geete. On this ridge, while the first infantry line from Orkney's troops was marching to reinforce the left centre of Marlborough's main body, the line of troops left behind remained on the ridge in full view of the Franco-Bavarians on the left bank of the river.

This manœuvre had the effect of making Villeroy believe that the whole of the troops under Orkney's command that had been attacking were still in front of his left wing, and it prevented him from reinforcing his centre from his left at this time.

So completely was Villeroy dominated by Marlborough's will and by his offensive operations, that he never attempted to make a counter-attack across the Little Geete in order to gain information and to obtain the initiative. He was content to ward off the attacks made on his position. It was evident that he had no clear idea as to how battles could be won.

He had not the intention of creating a favourable opportunity for resuming the offensive, nor had he any idea of swelling the number of troops available for offensive action in any one part of his position, as advocated in F.S.R. 88 (1):

> "The defensive, if an offensive spirit inspires its conduct, may effectively create a favourable opportunity for resuming the offensive, and may prepare the way for defeating the enemy when the general situation is more favourable. Again it may be necessary to remain on the defensive in one part of a theatre of war in order to swell the number of troops available for offensive action elsewhere."

Villeroy's command was weak and passive. His want of resolution in battle had the inevitable corollary of failure and loss of *morale*. [F.S.R. 11 (3).] His position, however, was strong, as his right flank would be difficult to turn. It rested on the River Mehaigne, and his left flank was protected by the marshy ground east of Offus and Autréglise, through which the Little Geete ran. This river would limit the power of movement and manœuvre of the enemy and would prevent them from making any counter-stroke which could not be foreseen by the Allies in position on the east of Offus. Also the Franco-Bavarian forces in this area could be contained by a comparatively small number of the Allies, so that superior numbers could be concentrated by Marlborough at a decisive point.

" Concentration of superior force at the decisive time and place, and its resolute employment in the battle are essential for the achievement of success."   [F.S.R. 2 (2).]

This concentration at the decisive time by Marlborough was facilitated by his dispositions made after a reconnaissance of his enemy's dispositions.   He saw that their lines were in a concave formation between Taviers and Autréglise, so that he posted his troops to face the Franco-Bavarians in a convex position, and then he could reinforce the centre, where he meant to make his decisive attack more quickly than his enemy could reinforce the centre from their flanks.

In this way, he would make the most of his numbers and would lessen the value of the enemy's very strong position. Villeroy, the French commander, in occupying his position, did not carry out the principles enumerated in F.S.R. (11):

" Unless the counter-stroke is to be carried out by reinforcements which have not yet arrived, the extent of the position taken up should not be so great as to reduce the number of men kept in hand for offensive action much below half the total force at his disposal."

Villeroy had his whole force of 132 squadrons, seventy-six battalions, and seventy-four pieces of artillery strung out between the River Mehaigne and Autréglise on a front of 6,500 yards, with no reserves in hand.

His isolated detachment of five battalions and dismounted cavalry, 1,500 yards east of Taviers, was too weak for serious resistance, and was too large for purposes of observation. Its use was a violation of the principle of economy of force.

In F.S.R. 59 (4) there is a warning as to the use of detachments: " They should be employed only in exceptional circumstances owing to the danger of their being cut off."   In this case, when at 1 p.m. the Allies began their advance, the five battalions and dismounted dragoons in Francqnée were soon surrounded and the village was captured.

On the northern flank, too, the Allies were successful; the Guards under Orkney's command had penetrated up to Offus, and had by their action occupied the Franco-Bavarian troops on their left flank, and had caused troops to be drawn from more important parts of the field before Marlborough withdrew them east of the Little Geete, in accordance with his plan of action.

Marlborough had not sufficient reserves to exploit Orkney's success.   He knew that he might have to draw on Orkney for reinforcements to enable him to carry out his main decisive attack, as his numbers and Villeroy's were practically equal. Actually this happened. The timely arrival of twenty squadrons drawn from his right flank turned the scale in Marlborough's favour in the final phase of the fighting on May 23rd.

Marlborough continued to maintain his objective with offensive operations on different parts of Villeroy's front.

After Francqnée was captured, he directed the advance on this flank to be continued to Taviers, in order to take advantage of his first success in following it up before the enemy in this quarter could be reinforced, and in order to prevent the French on this flank from sending troops to their centre, where Marlborough meant to make his decisive attack. He had made his plan and, as advocated in F.S.R. 77 (9), had decided on his main objective, on the necessary preliminary operations, on the direction of the decisive attack, and that penetration was to be aimed at.

Once Francqnée had been carried, and the French counter-attack had been driven back by the prompt action of Overkirk with the Dutch cavalry, the capture of Taviers on the left was the next operation, as in the possession of the Allies this village would cover Marlborough's left flank in his attack on his main objective.

Similarly, another preliminary operation was necessary before Marlborough drove in his decisive attack. This was the capture of Ramillies.

For this operation, Auverquerque led forward the Dutch cavalry. Schultz advanced with twelve battalions, supported by artillery, against this village at 2.30 p.m.

The cavalry charge up the slope between Taviers and Ramillies was at first completely successful against the first line of the enemies' cavalry. The infantry line, formed of twenty battalions on the ridge, was able to check the cavalry. This was an opportunity for the remainder of the French cavalry, who at once charged down on the Dutch cavalry as they were engaged with the infantry.

The momentum of their attack drove back the Dutch. It was then that Marlborough restored the balance of the fight by bringing the Danish cavalry from his right flank on to Auverquerque's left flank. In this, Marlborough showed his powers of leadership as defined in F.S.R. 11 (1); that is: " Personal courage, high intelligence, sound judgment, an intuitive faculty and great resolution."

He personally rallied the Dutch and was nearly captured in the ensuing *mêlée*. He brought to bear the full power of his force with his three arms acting in combination. [F.S.R. 12 (1).]

The whole of the British and Dutch infantry of the centre were sent forward against Ramillies supported by artillery, while the cavalry, brought from his right flank, worked round towards its rear.

The cavalry on both sides repeatedly charged each other, with varying results. The infantry under Mordaunt and Charles Churchill slowly fought their way forward until finally the Scots battalions were able to turn the scale in the favour of the Allies and to drive the French out of Ramillies.

The following principle, as laid down in F.S.R. 67 (1), was carried out:

> " The climax of every attack is the entry of the infantry into the main hostile position and the annihilation of the defenders in the hand-to-hand combat which follows the entry."

Villeroy had not foreseen the possibility of reinforcing his centre, and had to make arrangements when he saw his danger, and after Marlborough had brought his reinforcements to the spot where they were required. These reinforcements enabled Marlborough to have superior numbers at the decisive point, for, as the French were retreating from Ramillies, the Allied cavalry had driven back the French cavalry and were then able to charge the retiring infantry, while the victorious infantry, now that the enemy's main position had been penetrated, were able to turn against the flank of the garrison of Offus, which was still holding out. This was in accordance with F.S.R. 69 (4):

> " Penetration at one place only gives the attacker an opportunity of developing a flank attack against the enemy's defences."

The Elector of Bavaria tried to relieve the situation by sending in his available cavalry. They were charged by two British cavalry regiments as soon as they started, and were forced to retreat.

While the fight at Ramillies and on the ridge south of it was taking place, the Danes and Dutch worked round the south of Taviers along the River Mehaigne. By their occupation of the Tomb of Ottomond, the whole plain west of Taviers was dominated. Taviers was soon surrounded. When the attack from all sides was pressed, the garrison was forced to surrender, and the whole of Villeroy's right wing gave way.

G

The enemy's power of resistance had now been exhausted, and the whole French line broke up and retreated, closely followed up by the Allied cavalry, and, as advocated in F.S.R. 87 (1), the enemy were " allowed no respite."

Had Orkney's infantry, which had not been used in the first attack, now been available on the west side of the Little Geete, the demoralized enemy might have been destroyed.   The obstacle of the Little Geete and the morasses and ditches on either side of it prevented the infantry and artillery from carrying out the principles in F.S.R. 87 (5), namely :

> " Such infantry and artillery as are available should be despatched to assist that body of cavalry which is directed against the flank of the enemy's main force, with a view to completing its overthrow."

However, the British cavalry after the battle continued the pursuit till 2 a.m., when they reached Meldert, and then carried out the following principle in F.S.R. 87 (6) :

> " All pursuing troops should act with the greatest boldness, and be prepared to accept risks which would not be justifiable at other times."

Villeroy was not able to rally his army until he had re-crossed the Scheldt.

CHAPTER XII.

BATTLE OF OUDENARDE, JULY 11TH, 1708.

In this battle, the following principles of war will be considered:

Maintenance of the objective; economy; surprise; concentration and offensive action.

Maintenance of the objective. At a cost of just over 3,000 casualties, Marlborough defeated an army which was stronger than his by 20,000 men, at a cost to his enemy of 17,000 men. This was effected by Marlborough's maintenance of his objective.

His determination to fight the French in the open, once they had left their entrenchments and before they could reach a strong position covering Lille between Condé and Tournai, never wavered, in spite of the disparity in numbers of opposing forces in favour of Vendôme.

> "The essential characteristics of a commander are a strong and resolute will and a ready acceptance of responsibility." [F.S.R. 10 (2).]

Marlborough readily took the risk of sending Cadogan forward with a comparatively small advance guard to bridge the River Scheldt at Oudenarde.

He sent this comparatively small force ahead to ensure that they would reach the river in time to carry out their mission, as a small force would march more quickly than a large one. Cadogan's eight squadrons, sixteen battalions, with pontoons and thirty-two guns reached the river after a fifteen-mile march made in six hours. He was in time to intercept the advanced French troops before they arrived at Oudenarde on their way to Lille.

Throughout the day, Marlborough continued his offensive action, skilfully handling the successive detachments as they came up to the scene of action until he had established a line between Groenewald and Schaerken, and had driven the French right flank back to Browaan, and his troops had occupied the Boser Couter, which was a dominating position. Its occupation by the Allies made the French position untenable.

On the French side, this principle of maintenance of the objective was violated. There were divided counsels.

83

The Duke of Burgundy at first was undecided whether to oppose the Allies in their passage of the Scheldt or not.

Vendôme wished to attack as the Allies crossed between Heurne and Oudenarde. Burgundy, on the other hand, ordered the troops to halt as they were crossing the River Scheldt at Gavre.

The orders given by Vendôme then caused the seven battalions sent forward to cover his deployment behind the thirty squadrons, which he had sent forward to Eyne, to become an isolated detachment; their left flank was exposed to the Allies' advance guard crossing the River Scheldt near Oudenarde.

When the report was received at French Headquarters of this crossing, the commanders were not able to agree to any " definite plan or co-ordination of effort." [F.S.R. 2 (2).] Vendôme would not support his advanced troops, but decided to take up a position in the vicinity of Huysse, north of the River Norken, nearly 7,000 yards from the Allies' crossing-place.

Then, when this French detachment had been attacked and routed by superior numbers of Allies, Burgundy wished to retreat. Vendôme wished to advance. Actually, Vendôme's advice was acted on, and troops were sent down to Groenewald and Browaan, but too late to take the Allies at the disadvantage of disputing the river crossings.

The battle was fought at first round Groenewald, extending west to Schaerken as troops came up on both sides. Then, when the French right flank was driven back from Browaan, Marlborough completely enveloped them from a position farther west on the Boser Couter.

The principle of Economy of Force was violated by the French in sending forward an unsupported detachment to Eyne, four miles from Gavre, where the main body was halted When the French did advance, they did not continue their march towards Eyne, but went north-west to a position north of the River Norken, and away from their advanced troops.

On the other hand, Marlborough " economized strength while compelling a dissipation of that of the enemy." [F.S.R. 2 (2).] He sent forward his advanced troops to Groenewald, 4,000 yards north of where they had crossed the River Scheldt with their pontoons, in order to contain the Allies.

In this intersected and enclosed country, the guns and superior numbers of the French would not have full advantage, owing to the difficulties of observation and co-operation.

Marlborough was thus able to have in hand a force which he could utilize in the final decisive phase of the operations as soon as he realized that the French had given him a chance of gaining a decisive victory by leaving their right flank open by not occupying the Boser Couter.

The French in the fighting up to 6 p.m. had superior numbers engaged in frontal attacks. At 6.30 p.m., Marlborough carried out the following principle:

> "Concentration of superior force at the decisive time and place and its resolute employment in the battle are essential for the achievement of success." [F.S.R. 2 (2).]

As soon as Browaan, on the French right flank, had been cleared of the French, he saw that the Boser Couter was unoccupied, and that, if he could reach this position before the French could do so, he would be able to envelop their right flank.

> "The results of successful envelopment are overwhelming and usually decisive.

> "The delivery of an attack against an enemy's flank destroys his *morale*, drives him away from his communications, and implies the outflanking of such resistance as he has had time to prepare. Surprise should be aimed at if full effect from envelopment is to be achieved." [F.S.R. 69 (3).]

Actually, the French had not realized the importance of the Boser Couter and had made no effort to occupy it. Eugène took command of the right wing of the Allies' Army, and successfully pressed back the French past Groenewald to Royeghem, while the position of the British cavalry on Eugène's right caused the reserves under Vendôme and Burgundy north of the River Norken to be inactive.

Marlborough pressed forward, with the left wing now extended, to Bevere, which was taken by General Werk, commanding the Dutch Guards and the Nassau Wondenburg Brigades, while he sent the Danish cavalry farther to the west supported by all the available Danish infantry under Oxenstein in support, to make a wide turning movement to the west along the reverse slope of the Boser Couter, in order to gain a position dominating the rear of the French right flank.

This operation against the French right flank was in accordance with F.S.R. 70 (11):

> "Complete victory will be obtained only if reserve forces are employed to break down the enemy's resistance at vital points, and a commander must not hesitate to employ them in this way, even if resistance has not been broken down."

This movement on the Boser Couter was made unseen by the French.   As soon as the Allies were established on this commanding hill, they pressed on towards Oycke until they were round the French rear.   Then Marlborough ordered direction to be changed to the right, and by this time (8.30 p.m.) the French left had been encircled by Eugène's troops.

As predicted in F.S.R., the results of these movements were overwhelming and decisive.   It was only darkness that prevented the Allies from closing in completely on the French from both sides.

This advance to encircle both flanks became too dangerous, as there was a difficulty in distinguishing friends and enemies.

Vendôme did try to save the situation on his right flank, but the *morale* of his troops was not equal to the effect required to check the Prince of Orange and Tilly at the head of their victorious troops.

The French then carried out the principle stated in F.S.R. 87 (1), namely:

"The enemy may endeavour to break off the fight and withdraw before he has finally committed his force."

Vendôme was not able to utilize any of his forces north of the River Norken on his left flank, as they were watched by the British cavalry guarding Eugène's right flank.   This body of cavalry was ready to charge down on them if they attempted to cross the river.   Therefore, the French withdrew as best they could during the night; some went towards France, and the bulk of the Army went over the Huysse Hill towards Ghent.

Surprise, which is "the most effective and powerful weapon in war" [F.S.R. 2 (2)], was illustrated by the preliminary operations, when the Allies marched nearly thirty miles in less than thirty-six hours, and so were able to anticipate the French in their arrival at Lessines by July 10th.

The French cavalry then were surprised after crossing the River Scheldt at Gavre.   They advanced in a westerly direction quite unconscious of the presence of the Allied cavalry, who had crossed east of Oudenarde and suddenly charged them. This check to the French advanced mounted troops had an important bearing on the battle.   It caused the French commanders to reconsider their plan of action, and to decide on different courses.

Had their main force, then crossing at Gavre, rapidly continued their march, they could have disputed the Allies' passages of the River Scheldt.

The effect of their divided counsels was to cause a large

part of the French to take up a position north of the River Norken.   Seven battalions and thirty squadrons were sent forward to cover their deployment about Eyne.   Marlborough was thus given the advantage of crossing the river unopposed and then of fighting an encounter battle on ground which suited him and enabled him to make the most of his inferiority in numbers.   Finally, he was able to concentrate superior numbers at the decisive point and to defeat his enemy.

The seven battalions sent forward by Vendôme were later surprised and overwhelmed in an isolated position by twelve battalions of Cadogan's advanced troops at Eyne.   Cadogan's action in handling his advance guard to gain the advantage of surprising the enemy was in accordance with F.S.R. 47 (4):

> " If the commander of the main body has decided on offensive action the advance-guard commander should act with vigour against the enemy's covering troops and should secure any tactical points which may assist the development of the attack by the main body."

Cadogan knew that Marlborough's intention was to take the offensive, and accordingly he dealt vigorously with the enemy's covering troops, as F.S.R. state:

> " Such a step will rarely interfere with the superior commander's liberty of action, whilst hesitation and delay may do so by allowing the enemy to seize the initiative."

In the final phases of the battle, the principle of offensive action by which victory can only be won [F.S.R. 2 (2)], was exemplified.   Marlborough possessed in a greater degree than his opponents that " indomitable resolution and energy which enables the decision, once made, to be carried through." [F.S.R. 10 (1).]

He inspired confidence in his troops and maintained their *morale*.   In spite of his fatigue and the fever from which he was suffering, he conducted this difficult operation—the encounter battle—with all his usual skill and judgment.

In F.S.R. 11 (1) it is stated that:

> " The elements of war are physical fatigue, uncertainty and chance, and in no sphere of human activity do external influences tend more to distract man from his purpose and incline him to doubt himself and others."

In this battle, there were both uncertainty and chance, and Marlborough had to act without definite knowledge as to the enemy's movements and dispositions.

But he won the battle by maintaining the offensive throughout the day, and, as his troops crossed the River Scheldt and became available, he used them to prolong his left flank and to continue their attacks.

The first body of troops to follow Cadogan's advance guard were twenty battalions of British infantry under Argyle. These troops were sent to Cadogan's left flank to continue it towards Schaerken. The fighting was then carried on at close quarters in the enclosed country. The French in turn sent down more troops, who outflanked Argyle's left.

Marlborough then sent Lottum with Hanoverian and Prussian troops, as they came up, to prolong Argyle's flank and to check the French advance. He acted in accordance with F.S.R. 69 (1):

> "Decisions as to the plan of attack must be made rapidly. A commander will seldom be able to wait for full information as to the enemy's dispositions."

Eugène, with all available troops, was given command of the right wing, with orders to continue the offensive by driving back the French left flank. Marlborough's plan was simple and capable of being put into effect rapidly, as advocated in F.S.R. 69 (1):

> "The plan of attack must be simple. Under mobile warfare conditions it is generally better to carry through a simple plan than to await the results of detailed reconnaissance or to evolve an elaborate plan difficult to execute. The plan must be capable of being put into effect rapidly."

Marlborough throughout was undoubtedly helped by the weakness of the enemies' command. Their commanders pursued no definite policy and had no fixed plan, so that it could only have been by chance that they could have been successful. By attacking on ground unfavourable to artillery co-operation, with part of their force isolated at Eyne and part at Huysse, their plan was doomed to failure against an adversary whose "personality permeated his command" [F.S.R. 10 (5)], and who maintained "the impetus and offensive power of his troops." [F.S.R. 11 (4).]

The French commanders failed to support their advance guard and failed to concentrate their troops, although early in the day the time factor was in their favour, and they could have formed up either to attack Marlborough's army or to await his attack.

Their successive unco-ordinated attempts to deal with Marlborough and their want of resolution, led, as our Regulations state, to failure and loss of *morale*.

F.S.R. 69 (1) give another important warning as to the conduct of an encounter attack, namely:

> " Time is of the utmost importance.   The enemy must not be allowed to seize the initiative."

In this case, the enemy were engaged throughout their front, and, as they put in fresh troops to prolong their flank to the west, Marlborough continued the pressure by bringing up more troops to carry on the offensive on this flank, and, when the Allies' offensive had been successful between Groenewald and Schaerken, and had been carried forward with twenty fresh battalions between Bevere and Mooreghem to Diepenbeek, while Lottum's force gained ground towards Ruibroek, Marlborough " deployed the greatest possible strength for the decisive attack," namely, twenty battalions and all available cavalry of the left wing were sent round the reverse side of the Boser Couter, and were able to carry out an attack against the French rear.   This final offensive operation led to a complete victory.

The pursuit was taken up by forty squadrons at daylight on the following morning, followed later by thirty-four battalions, in accordance with F.S.R. 87 (1):

> " The pursuit must be taken up by as large a body of mounted troops as possible, so that the enemy may be allowed no respite."

Marlborough's main body, having marched over fifty miles since 2 p.m. on July 9th, and crossed two rivers before fighting a strenuous battle for seven hours, was naturally too tired to pursue after the fighting ended.   The Battle of Oudenarde closed at 9 p.m.

The French total losses in killed, wounded, prisoners and deserters were over 17,000.   Ten guns and nearly all their baggage and ninety-five standards were captured before their routed and demoralized army reached a temporarily safe position behind the Bruges-Ghent Canal.

CHAPTER XIII.

Battle of Malplaquet, September 11th, 1709.

The operations leading up to the Battle of Malplaquet opened with a surprise for the French. From Mons a road runs south-west to Valenciennes via Jemappes, and the Trouée de Boussu. Another road runs south from Mons to Bavai through the Trouée d'Aulnois between the Forests of Laignières on the south and the Forest of Taisnières on the north.

The French would have to march by one of these roads to relieve Mons.

Villars, commanding the French armies, decided to advance by the Trouée d'Aulnois. However, when his army arrived there on September 9th, he found that he had been forestalled by Marlborough, who had moved his force up from Quévy le Grand as soon as he heard from his advanced cavalry under Prince d'Auvergne of the direction in which the French were advancing. Villars was completely surprised when he found that the gap by which he hoped to advance on Mons was occupied.

Surprise may cause hesitation. Villars, luckily for Marlborough, delayed in his advance and did not attack, although he had superior numbers at the decisive point. Eugène's troops at this time were west of Quaregnon, Withers's detachment was still at Tournai, and the full complement of the artillery, even of the troops that were opposing Villars, had not yet arrived.

Villars did not know exactly what hostile troops were in his front, and he failed to maintain his objective when he was surprised by finding his road to Mons barred at the Trouée d'Aulnois.

Full information in war will never be available. A commander must make the best use he can of what he knows; and, in spite of doubt and uncertainty, must carry through his project. Hesitation and delay are fatal to success in war.

He was deceived by the vigour and energy displayed by d'Auvergne in the handling of his advanced cavalry. He thought that such confidence was the result of the close support of the main body under Marlborough. He consequently would not take the risk of pushing beyond the wooded country

90

in order, first, to gain the necessary information, on which he could base his plan, and then to maintain his objective by a bold assumption of the offensive.   This should not have been difficult, in view of his superiority of numbers.

In F.S.R. 29 (1) it is stated that:

" As the opposing forces approach each other collisions may be expected to occur between the respective protective troops covering the movements of the main forces behind them.

" Success in these initial combats will gain for a commander a general liberty of action, and will enable him to obtain further information of the enemy's strength and dispositions while concealing his own."

Had Villars acted boldly, in accordance with the principles laid down in this paragraph, he would have gained the necessary information, which would have enabled him to take the offensive with every prospect of success.   It would have given him liberty of action, as he could have reached open ground in which to operate beyond the Sart and Laignières Woods. Instead, he took up a position on the ridge between these woods.

Marlborough, on the other hand, directly he had heard from d'Auvergne that the French were in the vicinity, at once sent orders to Eugène to move from the Trouée de Boussu to the Trouée d'Aulnois, and he brought up his own troops at once to Aulnois.

Marlborough was prepared to take a risk, and Villars was unwilling to leave the shelter of the woods and the strong position which he could make between them.   He was unprepared to make a decision and to strike, although he had the advantage in numbers.   He did not carry out the following principle in F.S.R. 30 (1):

" The commander who first comes to a decision as to his course of action, and who gives effect to that decision without delay, will have the best chance of effecting surprise and thus forcing the enemy to conform to his movements."

Marlborough expected to be attacked at any time during the night September 9th/10th or during the next morning. Instead, Villars's troops were busily engaged in digging trenches in the Trouée d'Aulnois, and in strengthening their positions in the woods on either side of this trouée.

In F.S.R. 10 (1) it is stated that:

> " War is a contest between the will of the opposing commanders.   Success will be attained by the commander who possesses a greater degree of that indomitable resolution and energy which enables the decision once made to be carried through."

Marlborough's will was already dominating Villars, whose hesitation led him to adopt a passive defensive.   Villars did not carry out the principles laid down in the following paragraphs, F.S.R. 23 (4) and 24 (1):

> " The passive occupation of a position, however strong, can rarely be justified, and always involves the risk of crushing defeat.   A commander who decides to assume the offensive imbues his troops with a feeling of moral superiority over the enemy and compels the hostile forces to subordinate their actions to his.   The defensive entails temporary loss of initiative."

He was content only to drive back d'Auvergne's cavalry by sniping them from the woods.   The initiative thus passed to Marlborough, whose troops were soon in position within artillery range of Villars's right wing.   Having gained this advantage, it would appear that Marlborough's next step was clearly indicated: namely, to carry out a vigorous offensive with all available troops before the French had time to entrench further.   Every minute, their position could be seen to be made stronger, and its natural features were formidable obstacles.   Its flanks were concealed, there was room for manœuvre, and the ground over which the Allies could move freely in the open was limited to the gap of approximately 3,000 yards between the Laignières and Taisnières Woods.

Our Regulations state that:

> " Time is of the utmost importance.   The enemy must not be allowed time to organize his defences."   [F.S.R. 69 (1).]

On September 9th, Marlborough was not able to attack with reasonable prospects of success an enemy in such a very strong, sheltered position, as he had not had time to reconnoitre and to make his plan, and to allow his subordinate commanders to grasp fully his intentions and methods of attack.

> " Unless the plan of action is sound and has been carefully prepared, the highest moral and physical qualities on the part of the troops may be unavailing."   [F.S.R. 1 (2).]

Marlborough's army was in every way fit, but the time for careful preparation on the afternoon of September 9th would not have been sufficient to do justice to it in an attack against the French Army.

Our Regulations also state that:

" The efficiency of the leaders of the smallest units will often be the measure of an army's success." [F.S.R. I (2).]

There would be no time for information on all the important details, such as the main and subsidiary objectives, the direction and frontage of attack for each unit, the task of other arms in co-operation, and the orders for the attack to percolate through to the leaders of the smallest units, if Marlborough attacked on September 9th.

In addition, all the Allies' artillery was not up in position to support the attacking troops.   Marlborough could only hope to have the small superiority of twenty guns over his adversaries' eighty guns, and every help would be necessary for the infantry in their task of driving the enemy out of their strong positions.

Our Regulations are definite on the point of co-operation of the arms:

" In all operations there must be close co-operation between all arms engaged, the task of the supporting arms being to prepare the attack and to give the strongest possible support throughout every stage of the action to the attacking infantry, who alone can complete the victory by destroying the last remnants of hostile resistance. Infantry cannot advance against even semi-organized resistance unless that resistance is kept under subjection by fire power."

Also there would have been no time to co-ordinate a detailed plan in which the whole Allied force could co-operate, as Withers's force of twenty battalions from Tournai had not yet arrived.

Even after this reinforcement had joined Marlborough, his forces would only have a numerical superiority of six battalions over the French, and, though his battalions were the stronger in numbers, yet the numbers available on September 9th would not justify his attack on this day.

The further postponement of the attack by Marlborough on September 10th requires explanation.

The same arguments again are applicable.   In F.S.R. 23 (3) it is stated that:

> " Time is an essential consideration in deciding whether an opportunity is favourable or not for immediate offensive action."

In this case, it was essential to have every available man with the army for this deliberate attack.   Detailed plans for the co-ordination of all arms was necessary, and to obtain the information on which to base these plans, personal reconnaissance by Marlborough and his subordinate commanders was necessary.

Our Regulations state that:

> " Every commander should obtain by personal reconnaissance as thorough a grasp as time will allow of the ground over which his troops may become engaged and the topographical difficulties which they may encounter. The smaller the formation or unit the more detailed must this reconnaissance be."

To gain the necessary information, as to the extent of the French position, the weak parts of it, the obstacles to the advance, the best line of attack, the positions for the artillery, and the best forming-up positions for the attackers, would require considerable time, in view of the wooded nature of the country.

Withers's force was not yet up, and did not arrive until the crisis of the battle on September 11th.   On the previous day, in order to expedite the arrival of Withers's force and to shorten the march from Tournai, Marlborough attacked St. Ghislain successfully.

Also with his subordinate commanders he made a thorough reconnaissance of the position occupied by the French on the ridge in the Trouée d'Aulnois, and he was able to make an estimate of Villars's dispositions in the woods on either side of the trouée.   He saw the weakness of the salient occupied by the French troops in the Forest of Sart.   He realized the difficulty of making an attack east of the Forest of Laignières, owing to the marshy ground there, and that a frontal attack on the 3,000 yards of entrenchment in the trouée gap would be costly and difficult until the Sart Forest had been cleared and pressure could be brought to bear on the northern flank of the French centre, and that an attack on the troops holding positions in the Laignières Forest similarly would be costly and unwise until the attacks farther north had materialized and had shaken the defenders.

Therefore, Marlborough ordered the Prince of Orange, commanding thirty battalions, to contain the troops on the French right flank in the forest until the moment was favourable for pressing the attack.   Similarly, he was able to give detailed plans in accordance with F.S.R. 77 (9).

The first attack was to be carried out against the weakest part of the French position, namely, the salient in the Forest of Sart.   This was to be assaulted on two sides: from the north by Schulemberg, commanding thirty-six battalions, and from the east by Lottum, commanding twenty-two battalions.

Once the enemy had been driven from this wood, the French centre would be attacked from the north flank by all available troops under Schulemberg and Lottum, while Orkney, commanding fifteen battalions, pressed forward against the centre, and the Prince of Orange attacked Boufflers' force on the French right flank.

There was time for all ranks to know their objectives and what was to be done throughout the battle, so that co-operation throughout was ensured.

The line of advance for Withers was arranged through the Boussu gap, so that his force could strike the left flank and rear of the French when they were fully engaged on their front.

The point, however, that is open to adverse comment is whether Marlborough might not have remained in his position. Was an attack against an enemy so strongly posted and with time available to add to the strength justifiable with a numerical superiority of only 20,000 and twenty guns?   Mons would fall if Villars did not make an effort to save it, and the only way in which he could make this effort was by dealing first with Marlborough's army.

Marlborough would have then been able to strengthen his position, in order to hold it with the minimum part of his force, while the largest part was available for counter-attack. This would have been a sound plan if Marlborough could have been certain that Villars would attack.   Villars had allowed Tournai to fall without risking a battle; he might do the same thing again, and Marlborough knew that the capture of another fortress had not the same military value as the defeat of an army in the field.

He had few opportunities of dealing with the French field armies, and so he decided to take a risk.

F.S.R. 5 (4) states that " the choice of objectives must be governed mainly by considerations of policy " [F.S.R. 5 (3)], and of the " relative results to be obtained from success.   The objective which appears likely to lead most rapidly to decisive results should, as a rule, be selected." [F.S.R. 5 (4).]

Marlborough realized that the fall of Mons was not to be compared with the defeat of the last main French army in the field. The French seldom gave Marlborough the opportunity of fighting in the open. He was confident in the efficiency of every unit in his army, which reflected the personality of the commander. [F.S.R. 11 (3).]

> " It is the consciousness of knowledge which ensures self-confidence and enables a commander to judge situations on their merits rather than in accordance with any fixed formulæ." [F.S.R. 10 (3).]

Marlborough was confident, and his confidence in himself, in his subordinate leaders, and in his troops enabled him to take a risk, in order to obtain decisive results.

F.S.R. 24 (2) states that:

> " The offensive must not be assumed merely for its own sake. An offensive undertaken contrary to the dictates of sound reasoning will, if it fails, have a more serious effect on the *morale* of the troops than a wise decision to adopt a defensive policy."

Marlborough had no misgivings. He possessed the indomitable resolution and energy, which enabled him to make a decision and to carry it through.

Villars had occupied his position in accordance with the following paragraph in F.S.R. 92 (2):

> The distribution of troops must be designed " to ensure the protection of flanks and mutual support throughout the system. This principle must be applied not only to the infantry, but also to the artillery and other arms."

Villars had his troops distributed on a 5,000-yard front between the Chaussée Brunehaut in the Forest of Laignières in a north-westerly direction to the Forest of Taisnières.

The flanks in the two woods were concealed and strengthened, and the ridge in the centre of their position was strongly entrenched. The eighty guns were judiciously interspersed along the front, and were concealed in the woods being available to take in flank troops advancing against the centre. The position chosen did " permit of good ground observation and good concealment for the guns while denying those advantages to the attacker." [F.S.R. 89 (5).]

There was, however, no attempt to use the 260 squadrons, as advocated in our Regulations:

> " Cavalry must endeavour to mislead the hostile commander as to the exact situation and strength of the position, induce him to deploy prematurely and to fatigue his troops in groping for skilfully concealed flanks, and delay him so as to permit the defensive arrangements to be perfected."

In this case, they were massed in rear of the position north of Malplaquet.

They were to be used in the final phase to charge down on the Allied infantry when they were checked and demoralized by the fire of the defenders on the ridge in the woods.

The dispositions of the infantry were in accordance with the ideas of that time.   They were in lines covering the whole position.

> " All possible means must be employed to improve the natural tactical value of areas by the construction of well-sited trenches and by obstacles."   [F.S.R. 92 (2).]

Trenches were dug in the Trouée d'Aulnois and abattis were constructed in the woods.

Our Regulations also say that:

> " There must be sufficient local reserves in the hands of all subordinate commanders to provide for immediate local counter-attacks at all stages."   [F.S.R. 92 (2).]

Villars had the bulk of his troops in the forward lines.   On the right wing were only eight battalions in local reserve, and behind the left wing were seventeen battalions.

Of the remaining ninety-three battalions, thirty-seven held the lines of the right flank under Boufflers, thirty held the centre.   The remainder formed the left flank in the Forest of Taisnières.

Had Boufflers kept under his hand sufficient troops for immediate counter-attack he might have done more than check the attacks made on his line by the Prince of Orange when this commander had, at great cost, broken through the front lines.   He might have turned their disordered withdrawal into a rout before Marlborough was able to intervene and restore the situation with the Prussians and Hessians which he was able to collect.

H *

The situation had become critical for Marlborough, as his centre had been depleted to help his left flank, and Villars was preparing to take the offensive. Had Boufflers been able to take advantage of the disorder of the Dutch troops on his front, Villars's attack might have become effective before the arrival of Withers through the Boussu gap on the French left flank and rear. Reserves, however, were not available; Boufflers had not the time to collect any other troops to defeat Orange's force, and the favourable opportunity for the French passed.

Marlborough's conduct of the battle was as masterly as always. He inspired the troops with his own determination, and maintained their *morale*. He had the resolution and strength of will to force through the execution of his projects (*vide* F.S.R. 11).

In F.S.R. 67 (1) it is stated:

"There must be a good tactical plan, based on the best information obtainable; there must be secrecy in preparation, surprise in delivery; and skill and vigour in execution. In addition, there must be close co-operation between all arms and services engaged, the task of the supporting arms being to prepare the attack and to give the strongest possible support throughout every stage of the action to the attacking infantry, who alone can complete the victory by destroying the last remnants of hostile resistance."

In no battle did he display his military gifts to better advantage. His composure was unruffled even when he saw the grave danger to which his whole plan was exposed by the Prince of Orange's disregard of his orders. The mere sight of Marlborough riding at the head of d'Auvergne's thirty squadrons was enough to deflect Villars from his purpose at a critical time in the battle. This was when Schulemberg's attack had failed and a counter-attack by twelve available battalions against the flank of the attackers might have been the beginning of a rout of a large part of the thirty-six battalions, as they were withdrawing from the northern edge of the Sart Wood salient. Villars saw Marlborough, and counter-manded the counter-attack.

Prestige and moral effect are more "than half the battle, and the influence of the leader is chief amongst the moral factors that sway an army." [F.S.R. 11 (2).] Villars knew that Marlborough would have troops ready to deal with his counter-attack, and so great was his prestige and influence that he did not dare to risk an encounter in which Marlborough would be personally concerned.

Marlborough had a sound tactical plan based on the best information available.   It was first to eliminate the weak part of the enemy's position at the salient on the French left flank in the Forest of Sart, and then, having gained a footing there, to bring pressure to bear from north to south.

While he was trying to gain his first objective with thirty-six battalions under Schulemberg attacking the northern face of the salient, and with twenty-two battalions under Lottum attacking its southern face, both closely supported by forty guns, on the remainder of the front the French were to be contained by fifteen battalions under Orkney, and thirty battalions under the Prince of Orange, supported by twenty-eight guns.

Withers's twenty battalions were, during this time, advancing through the Boussu gap from St. Ghislain against the left rear of the French Army.   Also 2,000 men, drawn from the investing force at Mons, were operating in the woods on Schulemberg's northern flank.

Marlborough thus carried out, by his allotment of the infantry to definite objectives and arranging for their support by artillery, the principles laid down in F.S.R. 77 (3), namely:

"The knowledge of the enemy's dispositions and of the ground possessed by the commander will help him to decide at what point or points to direct his main effort to achieve the greatest success.   He will thus be able to group both his infantry and the supporting arms to the best advantage and to make detailed plans for sustained and overwhelming covering fire throughout the attack on those portions of the front where the attack is to be pushed home, and for sufficient covering fire to neutralize the enemy on the other portions of the front."

Marlborough posted his cavalry where they could exploit success [vide F.S.R. 74 (4)].   The attack started, as planned, at 9 a.m. on September 11th, with the advance to the assault of the troops in three lines, attacking the salient in the Forest of Sart under the supervision of Eugène.   Orkney and the Prince of Orange brought their troops into their allotted positions.   Schulemberg's first assault was not successful, owing to the stout defence of the Picardy troops.   He re-formed his troops, and at once returned to the attack, and, assisted by Lottum's troops, who gained ground across the Ruisseau de la Rulerie, was able to obtain a footing in the wood.

H2

Here, however, his troops were met by another line of entrenchments, and, in spite of much hand-to-hand fighting, were checked and driven back.

Orkney now took the responsibility of departing from the letter of the order given to him by Marlborough. He had been definitely told not to send infantry into the Forest of Taisnières. Our Regulations are definite on this subject. They are as follows:—

> " A formal order will never be departed from either in letter or spirit: (a) so long as the officer who issued it is present; (b) if the officer who issued it is not present, so long as there is time to report to him and await a reply without losing an opportunity or endangering the command."

In this case, Marlborough was at hand, and there was no difficulty in communicating with him; consequently, there was no justification for departing from the order. Orkney risked heavy loss of life, and he also ran the risk of compromising the whole plan by his further frontal attacks against troops behind entrenchments.

However, the attacks of his two fresh battalions did exert the necessary pressure on the enemy, so that Lottum was able to work his way slowly forward. Luckily the counter-attack by twelve fresh French battalions, as has already been narrated, did not materialize, as Marlborough was close behind with d'Auvergne's cavalry. Schulemberg and Lottum were able to press slowly forward on either side of the salient until the defenders gave way and gradually, by midday, were driven out of the wood.

Now was the time for Marlborough to carry out his offensive and to bring simultaneous pressure to bear on the front and flank of the enemy still in position at the Trouée d'Aulnois and the Forest of Laignières.

His plan was, however, by this time in great jeopardy, owing to the reckless disregard of his orders by the Prince of Orange. He had been ordered to contain by demonstrations the right wing of the French Army on his front. Instead, with his whole force he made a vigorous frontal assault against the enemy strongly posted in the Laignières Forest. At first, it was successful, though at great cost, in breaking through the enemy's first line of defences, and then the leading troops suffered heavily, as is prophesied in F.S.R. 97 (1):

> " If portions of an attacking force succeed in penetrating the defenders' position they will usually become more or

less disorganized owing to casualties and to the fact that they are operating on unfamiliar ground. The period of disorganization offers to the defender a fleeting opportunity for engaging the enemy when he is at a great disadvantage."

Orange's troops became disorganized after their heavy losses in the woods, where co-operation and intercommunication were difficult. Boufflers, with the reserves he had in hand, made an immediate counter-attack, and routed the Dutch troops. The Allied cavalry in the vicinity immediately carried out the rôle allotted to them in the attack in F.S.R. 74 (1): "To assist in covering the retirement of our own forces."

Twenty squadrons, under the Prince of Hesse, were at hand to deal with Boufflers' local counter-attack, but, before the Dutch troops were finally extricated, they had lost 10,000 men. Marlborough had posted his cavalry in accordance with F.S.R. 74 (3), and consequently they were able to intervene successfully in the battle. The situation, however, on his left flank was so critical that Marlborough had to deal with it personally with the battalions that he could collect. At this time, had Boufflers followed up his temporary success with all available troops, by making a deliberate counter-attack, he might have taken full advantage of the Prince of Orange's mistake and have gained a decisive result in routing the Allies' left flank.

In F.S.R. 97 (5) it is stated that:

"To judge the right time for changing from the defensive to the offensive is as difficult as it is important. The enemy may commit mistakes, such as exposing a portion of his force without hope of support from the remainder. These mistakes, all of which are favourable to the assumption of the offensive by the defender, may occur at any period of the engagement, even at the very beginning."

Boufflers, however, would not take the risk by making an attack, and Marlborough was able to re-establish the situation. Boufflers did not realize the principles laid down in F.S.R. 23 that "decisive success in battle can be gained only by offensive action. Every commander, therefore, must be determined to assume the offensive sooner or later."

In spite of the entreaties of his staff, he relapsed into the defensive, again behind his entrenchments, and the opportunity for further offensive operations did not occur again. Villars during this time had organized a counter-attack with fifty battalions, which he collected to deal with the advancing troops under Schulemberg and Lottum on the Allies' right wing. It was on the point of being successful, when Villars was wounded in the knee. A pause then occurred in the operations until he had been lifted from his horse and placed in a chair.

During that time, no orders had been issued, and then the French attack was not pressed. Time was now of the greatest importance to the French. Every moment was bringing Withers closer to their left flank, and was enabling Marlborough to re-establish the situation in front of Boufflers.

Villars's wound became more painful. He fainted and had to be carried from the field. There was no one present to take his place with the knowledge of the general situation and how Villars meant to deal with it.

Deprived of a leader, the French attack was not pressed. Eugène, though wounded, was able to rally Schulemberg's and Lottum's troops.

This was the opportune moment for Marlborough to continue his offensive operations in the maintenance of his objective. Villars had weakened his centre to strengthen the force with which he meant to counter-attack.

Marlborough ordered Orkney to attack with all available troops, and he arranged for his close support by artillery, and for the cavalry to be concentrated and ready to exploit the success to the full [*vide* F.S.R. 74 (3)].

Withers was directed to co-operate by attacking the left rear of the French Army. In this way, Marlborough concentrated every available man at the point where he would achieve success [*vide* F.S.R. 2 (4)] in an offensive against Villars's main force.

Orkney led thirteen battalions forward with the greatest possible determination, and was able to capture the French trenches in the Trouée d'Aulnois, closely supported by the Allied artillery, who from the forward position they had taken up were able to deal with the French cavalry in rear of the Trouée.

" Superiority of fire is essential to the successful conduct of the attack and artillery fire affords the most important means to this end." [F.S.R. 72 (1).]

When a gap had been made in the enemy's entrenchments, the cavalry passed through it. Their first attacks were successful, but they were driven back, and then the French cavalry, in following up the Dutch cavalry, were repulsed by Orkney's infantry, who were in the trenches which they had captured.

Whenever parties of Allied cavalry were driven back, they were able to re-form behind the infantry until Eugène brought up the last reserves and charged and routed the French horse.

On the French right flank, there was much hand-to-hand fighting between the opposing infantry in the Laignières Forest.

Again the cavalry intervened at a critical moment, when the Dutch infantry on this flank were giving ground. The Prince of Hesse-Cassel led his cavalry against the flank of the French from the south side of the Trouée d'Aulnois, and by 3 p.m. he was successful in checking the French right flank.

By this time, the cavalry had pierced their centre, and Withers, having advanced south of the Boussu Wood from close to La Folie, was attacking the left rear of their demoralized left flank. The French reserves had all been engaged. There was no alternative now for Boufflers but to save his army by retreat.

Marlborough had in six hours gained another very great victory.

This record of Marlborough's operations may suitably be concluded with a quotation from Alison:

" Marlborough was the greatest general of the methodical or scientific school which modern Europe has produced. No man knew better the importance of deeds which fascinate the minds of men; none could decide quicker or strike harder when the proper time for doing so arrived. None, when the decisive crisis of the struggle approached, could expose his person more fearlessly, or lead his reserves more gallantly into the very hottest of the enemy's fire. To his combined intrepidity and quickness in thus bringing the reserves at the decisive moment into action, all his wonderful victories, and particularly Ramillies and Malplaquet, are to be ascribed.

" But, in the ordinary case, he preferred the bloodless methods of skill and arrangement. Combination was his great forte, and in this he was not exceeded by Napoleon himself.

" To deceive the enemy as to the real point of attack, to perplex him by marches and counter-marches, to assume and constantly maintain the initiative, to win by skill what could not be achieved by force, was his great delight; and in that, the highest branch of the military art, he was unrivalled in modern times. He did not despise strategem. Like Hannibal, he resorted to that frequently and with constant success. Consummate address and never-failing prudence were the great characteristics of the English commander.

" He was often outnumbered by the enemy, and was always opposed by a homogeneous army animated by a strong, national and military spirit, while he was himself at the head of a discordant array of many different nations, some of them with little turn for warlike exploit, others lukewarm and even treacherous to the cause. But he never lost the ascendant; from the beginning of the war till his military career was closed in 1711 within the iron barrier of France by the intrigues of his political opponents at home, he never abandoned the initiative.

" He supplied, when outnumbered, the deficiency in military strength by skill and combination; when his position was endangered by the errors and treachery of others he waited till a false move on the part of his adversaries enabled him to retrieve his affairs by some brilliant and decisive stroke.

" It was thus that he restored the war in Germany, after the cause of the Emperor had been well-nigh ruined, by means of the brilliant cross-march into Bavaria, and the splendid victory at Blenheim. Thus he regained Flanders for the Archduke by the stroke at Ramillies, after the Imperial cause had been all but lost by the treacherous surrender of Ghent and Bruges in the very centre of his water communications."

APPENDIX

NETHERLANDS
THEATRE OF OPERATIONS

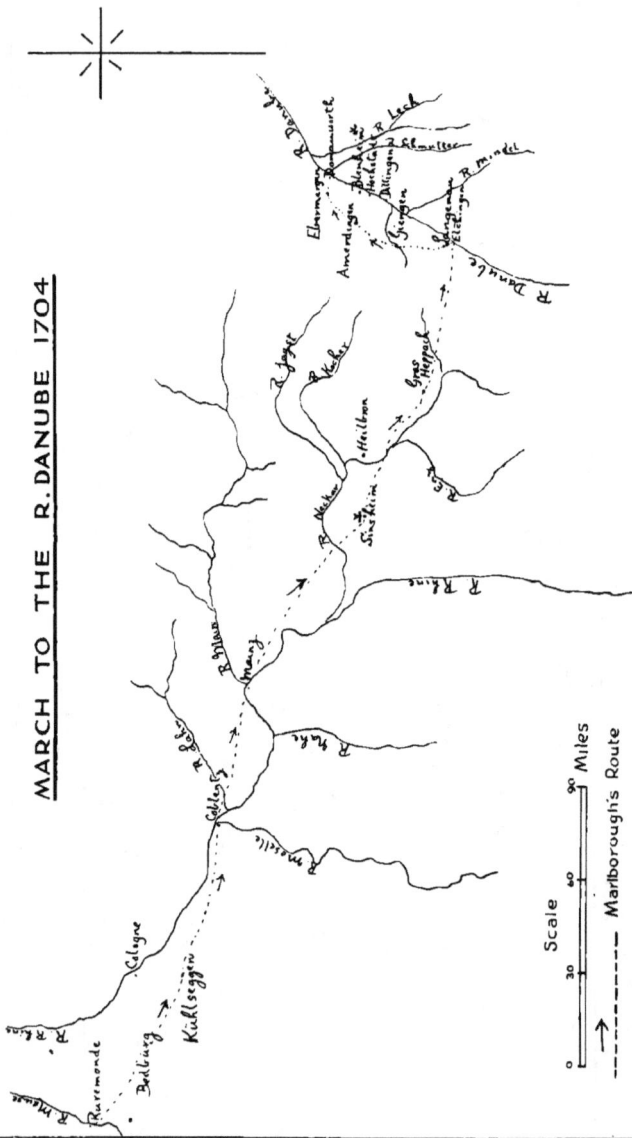

MARCH TO THE R.DANUBE 1704

Scale

0   30   60   90   Miles

-------- Marlborough's Route

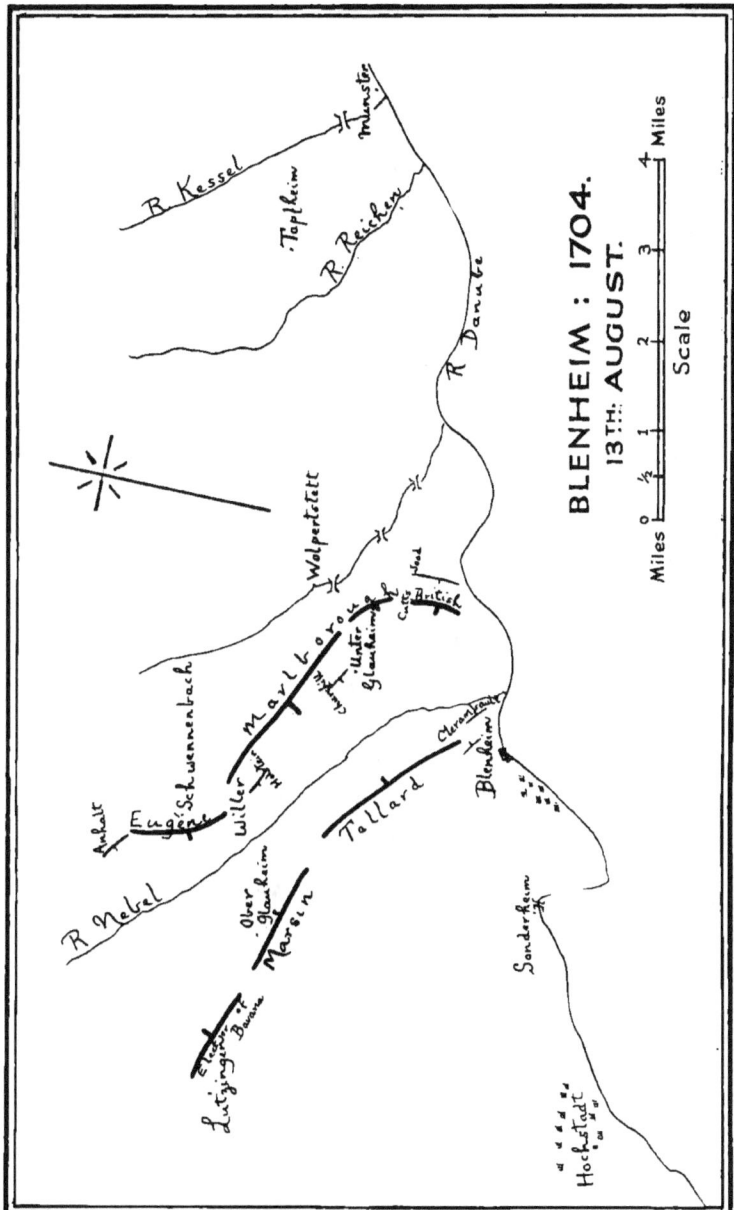

BLENHEIM : 1704.
13TH. AUGUST.

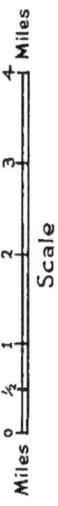

Miles |0 ½ 1 2 3 4| Miles
Scale

RAMILLIES
23ʳᵈ· MAY 1706

Great Geete

Little Geete

Mont St André

Autréglise

Fouly

General Direction of French Troops

Offus

Geest Gerompont

Orkney

Brigade

Lumley

Allies

Brigade

Ramillies

Tomb

Advance of Danish Cavalry

Tomb of Ottomond

Francqnée

Bonet

R. Mehaigne

Taviers

Miles — 0 ¼ ½ ¾ 1 1½ 2 — Miles

Scale

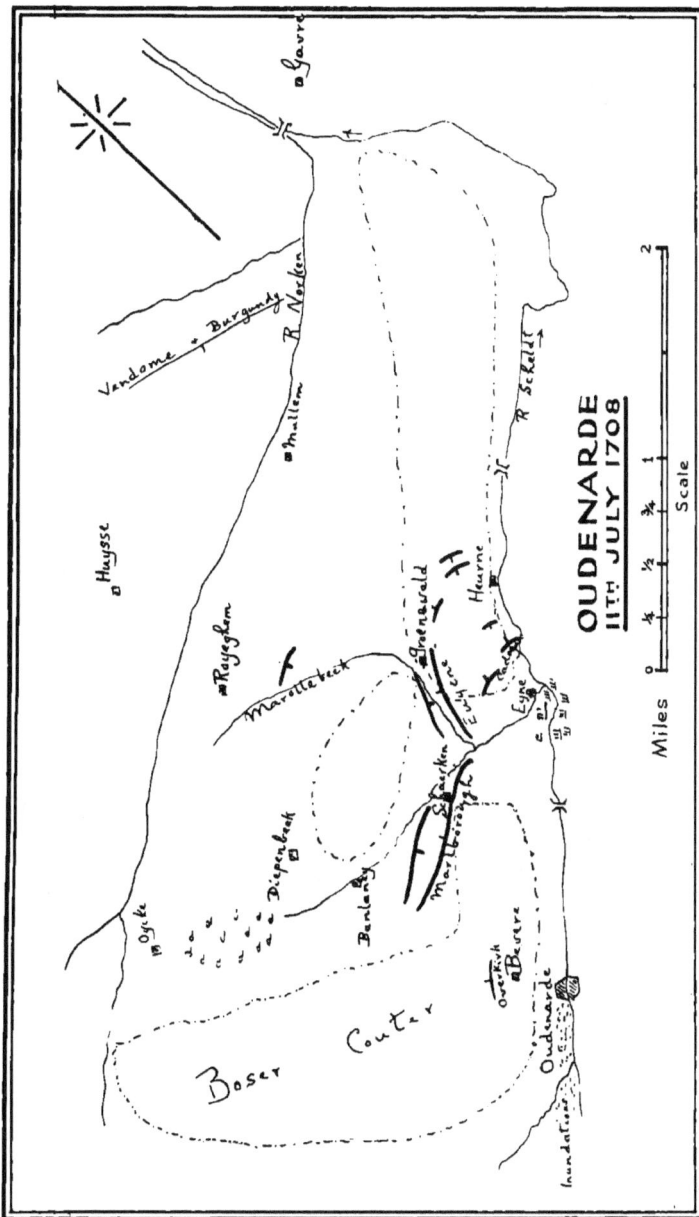

OUDENARDE
11TH JULY 1708

R. Scheldt

R. Norken

R. Marollebeek

Vandome + Burgundy

Gavre

Mullem

Huysse

Rayegham

Dieperbeek

Oycke

Benlaerg

Marlborough

Schaerken

Eyne

Heurne

Groenwald

Lyne

Oyckerk
Bevere

Oudenarde

Boser Couter

Inundation

Miles

Scale

0   ¼   ½   ¾   1   2

III

MALPLAQUET
11TH SEP. 1709

Scale

Miles 0 ¼ ½ ¾ 1 1½ 2

To Chaleroi

Blaregnies

Aulnois

La Longueville

Forest of La Longueville

Malplaquet

Forest of Taisnières

Taisnières

Camps du hamlet

Forest of Sars

Forest of Blaugies

Forest of

T. St. Ghislain

La Folie

Ruisseau de la Rulepte

To Mons

Hauteville

Louvignies

Sarsoy

From Bavai

From Bavai

112

INDEX